The Riddles of *Finnegans Wake*

The Riddles of *Finnegans Wake*

Patrick A. McCarthy

Rutherford • Madison •Teaneck
Fairleigh Dickinson University Press
London and Toronto • *Associated University Presses*

©1980 by Associated University Presses, Inc.

Associated University Presses, Inc.
Cranbury, New Jersey 08512

Associated University Presses
Magdalen House
136-148 Tooley Street
London SE1 2TT, England

Associated University Presses
Toronto M5E 1A7, Canada

Library of Congress Cataloging in Publication Data

McCarthy, Patrick A   1945-
    The riddles of Finnegans wake.

    An outgrowth of the author's thesis, University of Wisconsin-Milwaukee, 1973.
    Bibliography: p.
    Includes index.
    1. Joyce, James, 1882-1941. Finnegans wake.
2. Riddles in literature.   I. Title.
PR6019.O9F59356   1980   823'.9'12   79-24075
ISBN 0-8386-3005-7

Printed in the United States of America

For Florence L. Walzl,
with thanks

Contents

Acknowledgments	9
Conventions Adopted	11
1 The Riddle and *Finnegans Wake*	15
2 The *Ulysses* Riddles	33
3 This Nightly Quisquiquock of the Twelve Apostrophes: The Quiz Chapter of *Finnegans Wake*	47
4 The First Riddle of the Universe	78
5 Who's Who: The Prankquean's Riddle	105
6 Whose Hue: Izod's Heliotrope Riddle	136
Conclusion	153
Notes	157
Bibliography	168
Index	174

Acknowledgments

This book grew out of my 1973 doctoral dissertation at the University of Wisconsin-Milwaukee. My greatest debt is to the members of my dissertation committee, Janet E. Dunleavy, Roy Arthur Swanson, and Florence L. Walzl, for their help in shaping and revising the thesis. (The extent of my indebtedness to Professor Walzl, for this and other reasons, may be gauged by the fact that this book is dedicated to her.) I am also especially indebted to Phillip F. Herring for introducing me to Joyce's works in the first place, and to Father Robert Boyle for sharing his extensive knowledge of Joyce with me. For many helpful suggestions I particularly want to thank Bernard Benstock, and also Zack Bowen, Melvin J. Friedman, Adaline Glasheen, Gale L. Ward, and the late Mabel P. Worthington. Sharon Spiegel, who typed the first chapter, and Barbara Simons, who typed the rest, deserve special thanks for their excellent work under difficult circumstances, while Anne Hebenstreit merits thanks for her careful, intelligent, and sensitive editing of the typescript. Finally, I want to thank my wife Kitty and my daughters Keely and Cailín for making this project worthwhile.

Parts of this book have been published elsewhere: chapter 2 and a small portion of chapter 1 were developed into "The Riddle in Joyce's *Ulysses,*" which appeared in *Texas Studies in Literature and Language* (Spring 1975); chapter 3 was printed in the September 1976 *Journal of Modern Literature* under the title "Three Approaches to Life's Robulous Rebus in the Quiz Section of *Finnegans Wake*"; and a brief selection from chapter 4 was published as "Shem's First Riddle of the Universe Revisited" in *A Wake Newslitter* for April 1974. I want to thank the editors of these journals for allowing me to reuse this material.

In chapter 4 I have discussed some matters which are also treated in Leo Knuth's articles on Shem's riddle *(A Wake Newslitter,* October 1972 and December 1974). My initial drafts of this chapter were completed before Knuth's first article appeared, and the dissertation was accepted long before his second article was published. In the absence of a specific reference to Knuth, it should be assumed that I arrived independently at those ideas that are also included in his articles. I regret that Mr. Knuth's very interesting book *The Wink of the Word,* which includes material from the articles mentioned above, reached me too late to have any wider impact on the present study.

For permission to quote extensively I want to thank the Society of Authors, literary executor for the Estate of James Joyce, which holds world rights to *Finnegans Wake;* Faber and Faber, which holds world rights to the *Letters of James Joyce;* Jonathan Cape, which holds world rights to *A Portrait of the Artist as a Young Man;* and Viking Press, which holds the American rights to all three books. I also want to thank Random House, Inc., for allowing me to quote from the Modern Library edition of *Ulysses.* Finally, I am indebted to Clive Hart for granting me permission to quote in its entirety a detailed paraphrase of the "collideorscape" riddle that first appeared in *A Wake Newslitter.*

Conventions Adopted

Book and chapter numbers for *Finnegans Wake* are cited according to the formula II.3 for Book II, chapter 3. Page and line numbers for the *Wake* (21.18-19 for page 21, lines 18-19) are cited in the text. References to the marginal notes and footnotes in II.2 follow the formula 260.L1 for the first left-margin note on page 260, 260.R2 for the second right-margin note on page 260, and 260.F3 for the third footnote on page 260.

References to *A Portrait of the Artist as a Young Man* and to *Ulysses* are cited parenthetically in the text and are preceded by the symbols *P* and *U*. In the notes, all references to Joyce's letters are to the three-volume Gilbert-Ellmann edition, cited in the Bibliography.

The Riddles of *Finnegans Wake*

1

The Riddle and *Finnegans Wake*

Early in 1923, the year after the publication of *Ulysses* had shaken the literary establishment and permanently altered the shape of the modern novel, James Joyce began work on the mysterious book that was to occupy his attention for the next sixteen years. Refusing to reveal the ultimate title of the book to anyone but his wife, Joyce published occasional fragments under the running title *Work in Progress,* but within the book itself other titles or descriptions appeared: among those that survive in the final text of *Finnegans Wake* are "meanderthalltale" (19.25), "the book of Doublends Jined" (20.15-16), "this Eyrawyggla saga" (48.16-17), *"Rebus de Hibernicis"* (104.14), "this radiooscillating epiepistle" (108.24), "his farced epistol to the hibruws" (228.33-34), "a most moraculous jeeremyhead sindbook for all the peoples" (229.31-32), "Anonymay's left hinted palinode" (374.7), "Epistlemadethemology for deep dorfy doubtlings" (374.17-18), and "The last word in stolentelling" (424.35). In his letters Joyce described the book in equally enigmatic terms. In 1924, for instance, he sent Miss Weaver a key to ten symbols that he was using in the composition of *Finnegans Wake,* ending with □, which "stands for the title but I do not wish to say it yet until the book has written more of itself."[1] Three years later, his descriptions were not much more helpful: describing himself as an "engineer," he told Miss Weaver that "I am making an engine with only one wheel.

No spokes of course. The wheel is a perfect square."[2] Given Joyce's riddling descriptions of *Finnegans Wake*, it is hardly surprising that, whether they use the term to extol or to disparage Joyce's obscure dream-vision, critics generally have agreed that *Finnegans Wake* is a "riddle": Herbert Howarth called the book "a congeries of riddles"; H.G. Wells complained to Joyce that *Work in Progress* was composed of "Vast riddles"; and Campbell and Robinson began their classic "Introduction to a Strange Subject" by describing the *Wake* as "Running riddle and fluid answer . . . a mighty allegory of the fall and resurrection of mankind."[3]

That *Finnegans Wake* is a giant riddle is apparent to anyone who has made a serious attempt to follow even a page or two of the book. In fact, virtually any word, any description, any situation in the *Wake* resembles a riddle with multiple solutions. In this respect *Finnegans Wake* reflects the world it describes, a world in which rumor outdistances concrete evidence, in which appearance and reality are inseparable, in which the underlying order of human experience must be reconstructed by each person since the world presents such experience to us haphazardly and arbitrarily. Certainty is virtually nonexistent in this book of "wet and low visibility (since in this scherzarade of one's thousand one nightinesses that sword of certainty which would indentifide the body never falls)" (51.3-6). Throughout the *Wake,* order is buried under the appearance of disorder while, paradoxically, chaos lies beneath the appearance of order. In this sense, the riddling style of *Finnegans Wake,* which simultaneously reveals and conceals, is consonant with the dreamer's vision of "that sort of thing which is dandymount to a clearobscure" (247.33-34).

Joyce's scrupulous attention to answerable style in *Ulysses* is now legendary. On one occasion Joyce told Frank Budgen that he had worked all day arranging the words in two sentences,[4] and only a few months before the publication of *Ulysses* he wrote to his aunt, Josephine Murray,

Is it possible for an ordinary person [like Bloom] to climb over the area railings of no 7 Eccles street, either from the path or the steps, lower himself from the lowest part of the railings till his feet are within 2 feet or 3 of the ground and drop unhurt. I saw it done myself but by a man of rather athletic build [J. F. Byrne]. I require this information in detail in order to determine the wording of a paragraph.[5]

In *Finnegans Wake,* Joyce's stylistic problems were much more difficult than in *Ulysses,* but his determination to reproduce reality through language never weakened. Joyce believed that while we are awake we are constantly forced to make arbitrary distinctions in order to simplify reality and make it easier to deal with, but that the unconscious mind senses, however obliquely, the basic unity of all experience. In the mind of Joyce's universal dreamer, all myths become one: Finnegan's fall from the ladder, Parnell's fall from political power, and Adam's fall from grace are merely three variants upon a universal mythic motif, one that may be further illustrated through the demise of Humpty Dumpty and the cuckolding of Finn MacCool. Joyce's observation that in his works "the thought is always simple"[6] is true enough, but critics who have explicated aspects of Joyce's thought still find that the work itself remains an enigma that resists all forms of reductive analysis. Rather than offering an ultimate solution, Joyce forces his readers to think, to question, to doubt, and to work out the thread of correspondences that form the basis of "life's robulous rebus"— Joyce's riddle of human life (12.34).

In his use of riddles Joyce is not unique: the riddle is one of the oldest and most widely known of minor literary genres, and riddles appear prominently in the works of literary artists familiar with the genre as well as in folklore mythology. In its purest form the riddle is a complex or misleading metaphor. Aristotle noted that

> The essence of a riddle is to express facts by combining them in an impossible way; this cannot be done by the mere arrangement of words but requires the use of metaphor, as in "I saw a man by means of fire welding bronze upon another," and the like.[7]

Archer Taylor's definition is similar: "true riddles" are "descriptions of objects in terms intended to suggest something entirely different."[8] Perhaps the most famous riddle of this type is the Sphinx's riddle, which describes man as a creature that walks on four legs in the morning, two legs at midday, and three legs in the evening.[9] The metaphors in this riddle are simple: a cane is described as the third leg of an old man, and the stages in a man's lifetime—infancy, maturity, and old age—are described as parts of one day.[10] Any allegory that compares a short period of time to a longer one—the comparison of the Red Cross Knight's quest in *The Faerie Queene* to the entire history of Christianity, for example, or Joyce's comparison of one day in Leopold Bloom's life to a decade in the life of Homer's Odysseus—employs the same type of metaphor as the Sphinx's comparison of a day to a lifetime. The essential difference between the riddle and other forms of metaphoric or allegorical description is that the purpose of a riddle is to mislead and confuse the listener, at least temporarily, and to illustrate the ingenuity of the riddler.

Closely related to the "true riddle" are other types of difficult questions. Classified according to the relationship between question and answer, the most important of these varieties of riddles may be grouped in the following categories: conundrums and other witty questions; genealogical and arithmetical puzzles; and questions that are not meant to be answered, either because the questions make no sense or because they deal with the private experience of the riddler or require other arcane knowledge.[11] Examples of the conundrum, a variety of riddle in which the solution depends upon a fortuitous pun, include Athy's riddle in *A Portrait of the Artist as a Young Man (P* 25), Lenehan's *Rose of Castille* riddle in *Ulysses (U* 132, 134), and Mr. Bloom's question, "Where was Moses when the candle went out?" (*U* 729). The answer to the last of these, of course, is "In the dark."[12] A traditional conundrum that Joyce alludes to several times in *Finnegans Wake* is "Is life worth living?", which appears as an interrogative in "Was liffe worth leaving?"

(230.25) and "Is love worse living?" (269.F1), so that ultimately the riddle incorporates not only life but exile from Dublin and the Liffey, death, and love. In an early passage, the narrator suggests that it is the cyclic, repetitive nature of life—made possible by Anna Livia Plurabelle, the principle of renewal symbolized by the River Liffey—that makes life worth living:

> She is livving in our midst of debt and laffing through all plores for us (her birth is uncontrollable).... Gricks may rise and Troysirs fall (there being two sights for ever a picture) for in the byways of high improvidence that's what makes lifework leaving and the world's a cell for citters to cit in. (11.32-12.2)

A provisional answer to the riddle might be that life is worth living because of the individual's participation in the larger patterns that lend significance to life. Certainly Joyce seems to disdain the usual answer—"It depends on the state of the liver"—as an example of simple-minded concentration on the body at the expense of spirit. This answer, in fact, is associated with Shaun, who represents the gluttonous and materialistic aspect of mankind: he advertises his butcher shop with the phrase "His liver too is great value, a spatiality" (172.9).[13]

The genealogical riddle may be illustrated by Bloom's enigmatic self-description *"Brothers and sisters had he none,/ Yet that man's father was his grandfather's son"* (*U* 708). (I shall discuss this riddle in some detail in the next chapter.) The third group, riddles not meant to be answered, includes the nonsense riddle, a riddle in which the answer bears no logical relation to the question. Stephen's riddle about the "fox burying his grandmother under a hollybush" in the "Nestor" chapter of *Ulysses* (*U* 26-27) seems to be this sort of riddle. The group also includes riddles based on the personal experience of the riddler, such as Samson's riddle "Out of the eater came forth meat, and out of the strong came forth sweetness" (Judges 14:12-18). At times these riddles take the form of what Taylor calls the "neck-riddle": "The neck-riddle narrates an event known only to the poser of the riddle. By thus setting an insoluble puzzle the poser, who is condemned to death, hopes to save his neck."[14] Regardless of the circumstances, however, it seems clear that riddles throughout Joyce's works are never meant to be answered correctly, and that even if being able to create an insoluble riddle is not a matter of life and death, the posing of a riddle always represents a significant challenge of one sort or another.

One variety of riddle which seems particularly popular in Ireland is the triad riddle, a riddle with a three-part answer. This type is distinguished from all other sorts of riddles solely by the tripartite structure of the answer. Three of the fourteen riddles translated by Whitley Stokes from a fifteenth-century Gaelic manuscript are triads, and in their book on Irish riddles Hull and Taylor list twelve more triad riddles.[15] The general pattern of the triad riddle is illustrated by the following example, cited by Stokes: "What are the three dumb creatures that give knowledge to every one?/ Easy (to say): an eye, a mind, a letter." Hull and Taylor's first example of a triad riddle is even more interesting: "What are the three types of men that are best at deceiving (or: coaxing) women?—A handsome, unusual man; an ugly, witty man; a cripple (or: a bent man) who is wont to crouch over the fire." More often akin to witty questions than to "true riddles," triads are important because the answers tend to become proverbial: Vivian Mercier has noted that "Every saying in *Trecheng Breth Féni (The Triads of Ireland)* implies a riddle."[16]

Such a triad enters the mind of Stephen Dedalus as he parts from the smiling "Saxon," Haines: "Horn of a bull, hoof of a horse, smile of a Saxon" (*U* 23). Weldon Thornton has cited some possible sources for this proverb, all of which imply that Stephen is thinking of those things that are not to be trusted—an interpretation that is consistent with the context of Stephen's thoughts.[17] This proverb is probably derived from a riddle, or at least could easily be phrased as a riddle: "What three things should an Irishman distrust? Not hard to say: the horn of a bull, the hoof of a horse, the smile of a Saxon." If Stephen's triad refers to those things which we ought not trust (as the references to horns and hooves, associated with the devil, seem to imply), it is interesting that in the sixth chapter of *Finnegans Wake* two of the attributes of the hero Finn MacCool (alias H.C. Earwicker) are phrased in parallel fashion: "brain of the franks, hand of the christian, tongue of the north" (127.29-30) and "tronf of the rep, comf of the priv, prosp of the pub" (136.32-33). Later, after closing time at the pub, Earwicker is berated by the customers who have been ejected, and their description of the innkeeper—"Head of a helo, chesth of a champgnon, eye of a gull!" (377.4-5)—is a triad that reflects his initials, H.C.E.

Elsewhere, Joyce reverses the usual structure of the triad riddle by giving tripartite descriptions rather than answers: thus Earwicker is described in "shoots off in a hiss, muddles up in a mussmass and his whole's a dismantled noondrunkard's son" (125.1-2); "his first's a young rose and his second's French-Egyptian and his whole means a slump at Christie's" (130.30-31); and "my farst is near to hear and my sackend is meet to sedon while my whole's a peer's aureolies" (340.35-341.1). Like the Sphinx's riddle, in which the question is divided into three parts, and like the Prankquean's riddle and other riddles that are posed three times, triads lend themselves easily to application in *Finnegans Wake,* in which each stage of history (and of the life of the individual person) is divided, like the Christian Trinity, into three parts. Hence the tripartite descriptions above may be analyzed in relation to the cyclic life and death of mankind: in the third, for instance, "a peer's aureolies" puns on Persse O'Reilly, one of Earwicker's names in his role as fallen man.

The traditional riddle that Joyce seems to have found most useful in *Finnegans Wake* is the Humpty Dumpty riddle, which also illustrates Joyce's ubiquitous theme of the Fall. Versions of this riddle are widespread in English, and analogues may be found in many non-English cultures.[18] Many allusions to Humpty Dumpty in the *Wake*[19] establish this egg as one of Joyce's primary symbols for falling or fallen man:

> Have you heard of one Humpty Dumpty
> How he fell with a roll and a rumble
> And curled up like Lord Olofa Crumple
> By the butt of the Magazine Wall,
> (Chorus) Of the Magazine Wall,
>   Hump, helmet and all?
>
> (45.1-6)

Humpty Dumpty is a convenient symbol for proud, sinful man who rises above his station and, inevitably, falls. In a confessional passage, Earwicker reveals that his fall was that of Humpty Dumpty: "I, dizzed and dazed by the lumpty thumpty of our interloopings, fell clocksure off my ballast" (550.36-551.1). Humpty Dumpty's name refers to the hump which represents Earwicker's pride ("with a hump of grandeur on him like a walking wiesel rat," 197.3-4), his impotence (Anna Livia's husband is a *"much-altered camel's hump,"* 201.9), and homosexual tendencies (*"behounding his lumpty hump off homosodalism,"* 352.20). If the "hump" represents guilt, the "dump" is both the rubbish-bin of history that reveals the guilt of mankind and "that fatal midden or chip factory or comicalbottomed copsjute (dump for short)" in which Biddy the Hen finds the letter that implicates Earwicker in a nocturnal adventure with two girls and three soldiers in Phoenix Park (110.25-26). As an instance of the archetypal fall, then, Humpty Dumpty's fall is indistinguishable from Adam's, for "the umpple does not fall very far from the dumpertree" (184.13-14). Turning to Irish history, Joyce uses a reference to "the spell of hesitency" to equate the fate of Humpty Dumpty (alias "hasitense humponadimply") with the downfall of Richard Pigott, the Irish journalist whose forgery of letters supposedly penned by Charles Stewart Parnell was discovered when he was unable to spell "hesitancy" correctly (97.25-26).

In general, then, Humpty Dumpty's fall is that of Everyman. In particular, the fall of the egg represents the overthrow of the father by his sons: "Then old Hunphydunphyville'll be blasted to bumboards by the youthful herald who would once you were" (375.5-7). Butt, relating the story of how he shot the

Russian General (one of the more important allegories for the overthrow of the father), says "I shuttm, missus, like a wide sleever! Hump to dump! Tumbleheaver!" (352.14-15). In the *Wake* the fall of "Hump" (the father or, more generally, any authority figure) is signaled by thunder that ends one age within a cycle and begins another; at the end of a cycle the thunder signals the beginning of a new cycle. These thunder-sounds are indicated by hundred-letter words (what Adaline Glasheen calls "cletters") that appear ten times in the *Wake* (on pages 3, 23, 44, 90, 113, 257, 314, 332, 414, 424); the tenth contains an extra letter so that there are 1001 letters altogether—the number signifying renewal and the beginning of a new millenium.[20] In the seventh thunder-word there is a clear allusion to Humpty Dumpty or the fall of Hump into the dump: "Bothallchoractorschumminaroundgansumuminarumdrumstrumtrumina*humptadumpwaul*topoofoolooderamaunsturnup!" (314.8-9, emphasis mine). In view of Joyce's association of Humpty's fall with thunder, it is interesting that there is a Flemish riddle for thunder that is analogous to the Humpty Dumpty riddle. According to Taylor, "The notion that the egg cannot be made or repaired appears in the Flemish riddle for thunder, 'Holderdebolder ran over the storehouse. There is no carpenter who can make Holderdebolder.' The name Holderdebolder is used in Flemish versions of Humpty Dumpty."[21]

In accordance with the cyclic structure of *Finnegans Wake*, the fall is both end and beginning: the wake is also a breakfast and a communion; Earwicker is not only the corpse but also the meal; and both in the social and in the Eucharistic sense he is the Host. Hence, "even if Humpty shell fall frumpty times as awkward again in the beardsboosoloom of all our grand remonstrancers there'll be iggs for the brekkers come to mournhim, sunny side up with care" (12.12-15). More than universal man, Earwicker is the universe: Campbell and Robinson call him the "Cosmic Egg" whose shell is shattered while "the essential egg substance [is] gathered and served for the nutriment of the people."[22]

Given Joyce's penchant for reworking traditional materials, it is a little surprising that few of the riddling questions in *Finnegans Wake* appear to be based on traditional riddles. Aside from the conundrum "Is life worth living?" one major exception to this general rule is Shem's riddle, "when is a man not a man?" (170.5), which is obviously based on the widely known eunuch riddle and its many analogues, among them the "nobody and somebody" riddle for a mirror.[23] Elsewhere, in "Lindendelly, coke or skillies spell me gart without a gate?" (89.18-19), Joyce puns on an Irish version of a widely known spelling riddle. Explicating another passage—"Cardinal Lindundarri and Cardinal Carchingarri" (180.13-14)—Vivian Mercier has cited this form of the riddle: "Londonderry, Cork or Kerry, spell me that without a K."[24] As every child is aware, the trick lies in knowing which word to spell; the solution is "t-h-a-t." I have found no traditional riddles that are analogous to other riddling questions in *Finnegans Wake,* although it is possible that some of them are based on folk riddles that have not yet been collected. More often, the *Wake* riddles have the appearance of traditional riddles or incorporate some of the characteristics of folk riddles. Jaun's "What's overdressed if underclothed?" (441.5) takes the form of a paradoxical riddle like the eunuch riddle, but in another sense it is simply an expression of Jaun's incestuous lust for his sister, Issy: as far as he is concerned, she is overdressed even when underclothed (or clad only in her underclothes). The Finn MacCool riddle (126.10-139.14), on the other hand, parodies the convention of listing the attributes of the object described in a riddle by carrying on the list for thirteen pages, and the chapter that begins with this riddle is an extended riddle contest that symbolizes the struggle of the opposing forces represented by the brothers Shem and Shaun.

Although none of the riddling questions in the *Wake* alludes to the Sphinx's riddle, one of Earwicker's self-descriptions does: "God serf yous kingly, adipose rex! I had four in the morning and a couple of the lunch and three later on"

(499.16-17). (It is also possible that some or all of the references to 432, which alludes primarily to the date traditionally cited for the beginning of St. Patrick's mission in Ireland, form permutations on the 4-2-3 pattern of the Sphinx's riddle.) Other references to the Sphinx's riddle include "whenever it was he reddled a ruad to riddle a rede from the sphinxish pairc" (324.6-7) and "Afeared themselves were to wonder at the class of a crossroads puzzler he would likely be" (475.3-4). While allusions to the Humpty Dumpty riddle are also scattered throughout the *Wake,* they too never take the form of riddling questions with which one character hopes to stump another; the importance of this riddle in *Finnegans Wake* derives solely from the rich symbolic associations attached to the egg and its relation to the Fall of Man. Other important themes and symbols in the *Wake* may also owe something to particular riddles: Joyce's concern with the death that produces life may be related to Claret's Latin riddle for a seed,[25] and the relationship between Anna Livia Plurabelle (represented by the River Liffey) and her daughter, a cloud, is analogous to Claret's *"Quam genetrix genuit, genetricem nata regignit./ Unda fit in glaciem, glacies in aquam fit ibidem"* ("Mother gives birth to daughter, and daughter again to mother.—Water is changed into ice, and ice likewise into water").[26] Since the themes and symbols cited here are traditional and widely recognized, however, it seems unlikely that Joyce's handling of these symbols is derived specifically from Claret's riddles; rather, the most that can be said with any assurance is that both Joyce and Claret found in the symbol of the seed and in the relationship between water and its nonliquid forms the important theme of the cyclic repetition of life.

Ward Swinson has observed that "the riddler who propounds a riddle which no one can answer assures for himself a reputation for the highest wisdom and a position of ultimate power in the society," and that "Joyce connected riddles with knowledge, power and the creative artist."[27] As he points out, Athy, who poses a riddle that Stephen cannot answer, is "shown to be the possessor of secret knowledge denied to the other boys" when he tells the others that a number of boys are being expelled or flogged for a homosexual offense.[28] Another apparent bearer of secret knowledge in this passage (*P* 40–42) is Wells, who claims that the boys are being punished for stealing and drinking altar wine. Earlier, Wells asked Stephen whether or not he kissed his mother at night; Stephen first answered yes and then no, but both times Wells and the others laughed. Stephen thought, "What was the right answer to the question? He had given two and still Wells laughed" (*P* 14). In *Ulysses,* Stephen (like Blake's Los, who knew that he must create his own system or be enslaved by another man's) tries his hand at setting riddles: in the "Nestor" chapter he poses riddles in order to retain his control over his classroom. In *Finnegans Wake,* again, the Prankquean, Shem, and other characters propound riddles that are supposed to establish them as the bearers of arcane knowledge. As Huizinga has noted, such knowledge is very important:

> For archaic man, doing and daring are power, but knowing is magical power. For him all particular knowledge is sacred knowledge—esoteric and wonder-working wisdom, because any knowing is directly related to the cosmic order itself.[29]

In folklore and written narratives, the power of the riddle is illustrated by the use of riddles as challenges or tests. An interesting example of the use of riddles as a challenge has been cited by Fred Norris Robinson. In this medieval Irish story Marban, a hermit and poet, decided to take revenge on a group of poets who plagued Marban's brother, their host, with impossible demands, so he required each of them to sing a *cronán* ("a low humming tune") until he had heard as much as he desired. The task was so difficult that "Efforts were made to put off Marban with riddle contests, but he always defeated his antagonists in questions, and then reverted to his first demand."[30] Even more common is the use of riddles as tests for heroes (as in some versions of the Grail quest). Taylor, for example, has cited three riddles from the tenth-century Persian epic *Shahnameh*, in which the emperor tests the fitness of the hero, Zal, by requiring him to answer cosmological riddles.[31] On the other hand, the fact that the ability to answer riddles is commonly seen as evidence of a heroic future invests the story of Oedipus with irony, since Oedipus is able to solve the riddle for man but is unable to see himself clearly—to understand individual man.

In folklore generally, and particularly in Irish narratives, riddles are often employed as suitor tests—tests in which the would-be husband is required to perform a feat, answer a question, or pass some other test in order to win a bride.[32] This special use of riddles is important in *Finnegans Wake*, for it demonstrates why riddles play such a prominent role in The Tale of Jarl van Hoother and the Prankquean (21-23) and in The Mime of Mick, Nick and the Maggies (219-59). (I shall discuss these episodes in later chapters.) In English literature the most familiar use of a riddling test for a suitor is the casket test in *The Merchant of Venice:* the Prince of Morocco and the Prince of Arragon misinterpret the enigmatic inscriptions on the caskets and choose wrongly before Bassanio, choosing the lead casket with the inscription "who chooseth me must give and hazard all he hath," finds Portia's image inside.[33] The use of riddles as suitor tests in Irish literature may be illustrated by Mercier's reference to an Irish story in which "the courtship of Finn and the maiden Ailbe is carried on by means of riddles"; Mercier also reprints part of an analogous riddling conversation between Cuchulain and Emer.[34] The popularity of this motif in Irish literature not only reflects the Irish love of wit but suggests that, for the Irish, wordplay is more than mere play: it is also a test of the intellect, and more generally a test of one's fitness for any of a number of serious purposes.

There is however one sense in which solving riddles may be a very dangerous undertaking, for riddling is often associated with incest. Anthony Burgess, who has made this association the basis for his novel *MF,* has called attention to part of a lecture delivered by Claude Lévi-Strauss at the College de

France in 1960.[35] Lévi-Strauss relates a myth, found among the Iroquois and Algonquin Indians, that involves both riddling and incest. Through a structural comparison of this story with the myth of Oedipus, Lévi-Strauss attempts to prove that solving a riddle is the grammatical equivalent of committing incest. His conclusion is that "Like the solved puzzle, incest brings together elements doomed to remain separate: the son marries the mother, the brother marries the sister, *in the same way in which the answer succeeds, against all expectations, in getting back to its question.*"[36] Because Oedipus and other riddle-solvers violate the tenuous order of the universe, they may spawn pestilence. On this level, then, it may be seen that in *Finnegans Wake* the dreamer's fascination with riddles parallels his incestuous desires, and that his refusal to answer his own questions represents his attempt to avoid the fate of Oedipus.

Lévi-Strauss's structuralist interpretation of the riddle-incest relationship closely parallels Joyce's allegorical interpretation: in *Finnegans Wake* both incest and riddling relate to the Fall of Man and the theme of forbidden knowledge. While the riddles deal in many ways with the knowledge of good and evil, incest represents forbidden carnal knowledge—and Issy, the apple of her father's eye (372.3), is the forbidden fruit. Since on one level Earwicker is identified with the dreamer, the riddles are (like his daughter) his own creation, and his refusal to answer them parallels his refusal to "know" his daughter. Clearly Jarl van Hoother, slamming the door on the Prankquean, is attempting to avoid an incestuous relationship; one of many possible interpretations of the Prankquean's riddle ("why do I am alook alike a poss of porterpease?"—21.18-19) is that it is the daughter's malicious attempt to force the poor man to admit that the temptress is his look-alike because they are both members of the Porter family. Izod's "heliotrope" riddle in II.1 is even more obviously a temptation to commit an incestuous act, since the answer to the riddle is also the color of her underpants. Like the Prankquean episode, too, the episode of the Mime reproduces the nebulous Phoenix Park incident in which Earwicker was involved in a minor act of sexual indiscretion with two girls who are a dual representation of the daughter. The exact nature of this incident is perhaps the ultimate riddle of the *Wake;* certainly the dreamer's twin desires to discover precisely what happened and to avoid the subject altogether suggest the riddle's importance both as a sign of power and as dangerous or forbidden knowledge. The association of riddling and incest extends to the Finn MacCool riddle, which includes several references to the Park incident, and to Shem's "when is a man not a man?" riddle which refers in part to Earwicker's "unmanly" desire for sexual union with his daughter.

Joyce's fascination with riddles in *Finnegans Wake* derives partly from his interest in the hermetic nature of the universe.[37] Like metaphor and allegory, the "true riddle" establishes correspondences between apparently dissimilar people, objects, events, or processes. In the *Wake* it is axiomatic that nothing is new; rather, current events follow patterns established in prehistoric times, each generation acting out familiar roles based on family relationships. (The fact that all the characters in the book are members of one family helps to explain why every riddle that is part of a suitor test must involve incest.) The universalization of character that Joyce insists on makes it possible to see every authority figure in the father, every rebel in Shem, every bourgeois moralist in Shaun; furthermore, the characters are indistinguishable from the elemental patterns of the book, so that the Four Old Men are not only the judges at the trial of Festy King but also the four evangelists, the four provinces of Ireland, the authors of *The Annals of the Four Masters,* the four ages of history (golden, silver, copper, iron), the four elements, and even the four posts of the bed in which Mr. and Mrs. Porter, alias H.C.E. and A.L.P., lie. Correspondences between Earwicker's family and historic personages are often complex and the world of *Finnegans Wake* is constantly in flux, but the constant reappearance of archetypal patterns is Joyce's proof that everything under the sun is merely "the seim anew" (215.23). When we decipher the correspondences and riddling descriptions, finding that a hermit wading in a stream is also a man having intercourse with a woman and that a rock and a tree are also Saints Peter and Paul, we begin to experience the hermetic nature of Joyce's dream-world, in which everything assumes significance by virtue of its correspondence to something else.

Even in his puns Joyce resembles a riddler, for Gaelic riddles frequently depend for their effect upon highly sophisticated puns.[38] Joyce's concept of the creative artist seems always to involve some form of riddle: the riddler is the equivalent of the Daedalean artificer, for the riddle is a form of verbal labyrinth whose purpose is to puzzle or mislead. Moreover, as Huizinga notes, "As a form of competition proper, archaic poetry is barely distinguishable from the ancient riddle-contest."[39] He observes that

> The close connections between poetry and the riddle are never entirely lost. In the Icelandic *skalds* too much clarity is considered a technical fault. The Greeks also required the poet's word to be dark. Among the troubadours, in whose art the play-function is more in evidence than in any other, special merit was attributed to the *trobar clus*—the making of recondite poetry.[40]

In view of Henry Frank Beechhold's demonstration that Joyce thought of himself as part of the Gaelic poetic tradition— specifically, as an *ollave* or *fili*[41]—it is significant that in the archaic Irish poetic tradition the formula *Ni ansa*, "Not hard (to say)," is not only the traditional formula for beginning the answer to a riddle but also the formula for beginning the recitation of a story that is prefaced by a question.[42] Joyce's deviation from this tradition consists, in part, in treating his materials on two levels, both as universal knowledge that is accessible to everyone and as obscure knowledge that is clear to no one: *Ni ansa* sounds enough like "No answer" for Joyce to transmute it into "Noanswa" (23.20-21; cf. 105.14).

Like a riddle, *Finnegans Wake* derives much of its power from its ability to baffle us, to lead us into the search for answers that are never wholly satisfying. Taylor has reprinted a riddle (in the form of a sonnet) by Galileo Galilei that describes "a monster that is rendered powerless by knowing its name—a comparison which was suggested by the story of the Sphinx."[43] The answer, of course, is "a riddle," since riddles lose their power when they are solved. Like Rumpelstiltskin, who lost his right to the Queen's first-born child when the Queen learned his name, and Odysseus, who was nearly killed by the Cyclops when he abandoned his pseudonym "Noman" and revealed his true name, the riddler risks losing all if his riddle is solved. Like Jehovah, who would not allow his name to be pronounced, Joyce kept the title of *Finnegans Wake* secret through the sixteen years of *Work in Progress*. Indeed, like God, *Finnegans Wake* eludes referential definition, and when Tindall answers that annoying question "what is *Finnegans Wake* all about?" by saying that *"Finnegans Wake* is about *Finnegans Wake,"*[44] he instinctively defines Joyce's circular book in terms that recall God's circular self-definition: "I AM THAT I AM" (Exodus 3:14). Although what we know about *Finnegans Wake* has already filled many volumes, there is much more that we do not know and much, indeed, that we will never know. As Mrs. Glasheen has noted,

> *Finnegans Wake* is a model of our universe as we perceive it. It is mysterious as a whole and in its parts; Joyce imitates God and is mysterious in his turn. It is not true to say that *Finnegans Wake* is mysterious because of Joyce's great learning, and could we but duplicate that learning, did we know Vico and seventeen languages—why then the book would be plain as a pike-staff. No. *Finnegans Wake* is wilfully obscure. It was conceived as obscurity, it was executed as obscurity, it is about obscurity.[45]

The *Wake* is not altogether obscure, of course, but no explication ever seems complete: the reader who sees a reference to the Battle of Clontarf (fought in 1014) in "Clontarf, one love, one fear" (324.20–21) is right, but on another level the phrase is meant to be a telephone number: CL 1014.[46] (The phrase also alludes to monogamy, since Gaelic *fear* means "man.") Although on occasion Joyce disclaimed any interest in the "meaning" of *Finnegans Wake,* at other times he thought of the book as a puzzle for the reader to solve: in 1925 he wrote to Harriet Shaw Weaver, saying "I put in a few more puzzles into my piece,"[47] and he was fond of offering explications of individual words and phrases. The facsimile publication of all of the *Finnegans Wake* manuscripts, notebooks, and proofs threatens to increase many times over the amount of evidence that a *Wake* scholar must wade through to come to grips with the text, but from what we already know of the book it is clear that there will be no "definitive solution" forthcoming—just an increased appreciation of the beauty and coherence of Joyce's "meanderthalltale." Like the macrocosm and the microcosm that it imitates—the universe and the human mind—*Finnegans Wake* will never be fully explicated, but the pleasure of solving one part of the puzzle, putting one more piece into place, makes the effort worthwhile.

In the following chapters, then, I am going to try to put a few pieces into place by exploring Joyce's treatment of specific riddles and riddle situations. After a brief commentary on the riddles in *Ulysses,* I shall turn my attention to three riddles in the "quiz" section (I.6), and then to Shem's riddle, the Prankquean's riddle, and the "heliotrope" riddle. Since the riddle is a model of *Finnegans Wake,* it is my contention that these particular riddles are especially important passages that deserve close analysis for the light they can shed on the *Wake* as a whole.

2

The *Ulysses* Riddles

The riddles in *Ulysses* are in some respects a key to the riddles in *Finnegans Wake:* in both works major themes, especially those dealing with a character's understanding of his identity, are expressed through riddles. Even in *A Portrait of the Artist as a Young Man,* Joyce used riddles to develop his themes: Athy's riddle, "Why is the county Kildare like the leg of a fellow's breeches?" (*P* 25), and the crocodile's question in Cranly's story (*P* 250) are obvious examples. As Tindall has noted, Joyce's fascination with "the unanswerable question" led him to "put riddles into all his major works, which . . . seem riddles, too."[1] In *Ulysses* Joyce experimented with the riddle, exploring its symbolic potential and discovering within this one device a myriad of uses. The elusiveness of the riddle solution (reflecting Joyce's distrust of appearances and certainty) and the reliance on contrived or artificial correspondences relate the riddle to the thematic and technical bases of Joyce's fluid allegory. While all answers to Joycean riddles are provisional, certain important elements of Joyce's technique may be illustrated through a comparative study of Stephen Dedalus's riddles in the "Nestor" chapter (a highly concentrated set of symbolic expressions of ideas that plague Stephen throughout the day) and Lenehan's *Rose of Castille* riddle (a statement of one of the more significant motifs associated with Bloom). A study of these riddles will demonstrate both the technical diversity and the thematic unity of the *Ulysses* riddles, for in quite different ways the riddles posed by Stephen and Lenehan deal with crucial problems of identity and human relationships.

While these passages are most significant to an understanding of riddles in *Ulysses* and the *Wake,* it should be noted that there are many more riddling questions in *Ulysses.* At the end of the day, for example, Bloom recalls a "selfinvolved enigma" that he still has not solved and a "selfevident enigma" that, after thirty years of pondering, he has finally solved: "Who was M'Intosh?" and "Where was Moses when the candle went out?" (*U* 729). (In a sense both of these enigmas are "selfinvolved" since M'Intosh and Moses are keys to Bloom's symbolic identities.) Elsewhere in the same chapter, Bloom identifies himself through a variation upon one of the most familiar genealogical riddles: *"Brothers and sisters had he none,/ Yet that man's father was his grandfather's son"* (*U* 708). Even Molly knows a riddle, a bawdy one that she overheard one day while passing by some boys on a street corner: " . . . my uncle John has a thing long . . . my aunt Mary has a thing hairy . . . and he puts his thing long into my aunt Marys hairy etcetera and turns out to be you put the handle in a sweepingbrush" (*U* 776-77). Molly's riddle is a variant on a traditional metaphoric riddle that appears in the West Indies in the following form: "My father, John take the long long t'ing and he shove it a Mary hairy-hairy.— Broom."[2] Molly's riddle is sexually suggestive, while Bloom's riddles seek to establish his identity: the main purpose of these riddles seems to be to illustrate some facets of the characters of Mr. and Mrs. Bloom.

Stephen's riddles in "Nestor," however, are more: they are highly compressed symbolic revelations of Stephen's state of mind. The "Nestor" episode has its setting in Mr. Deasy's school, where Stephen conducts class, dismisses the boys, and collects both his wages and some unsolicited advice from Mr. Deasy. Early in the chapter, Stephen's musings on Christ's "riddling sentence," "To Caesar what is Caesar's, to God what is God's" (*U* 26), illustrate one function of riddles here and elsewhere in Joyce's works: like Christ's evasive reply, a riddle may be used as a defense mechanism, designed to conceal meaning rather than to reveal it. Stephen's spoken riddles, which the students cannot answer, are used defensively: Stephen hopes that by stumping his students he can maintain his superior position within the classroom. This point is illustrated by Stephen's question about a pier, which, while not strictly a riddle, involves the elements of figurative description and complexity that are associated with the true riddle. Stephen has asked Armstrong a question about Pyrrhus and in response has received a joke: "Pyrrhus, sir? Pyrrhus, a pier." Amid the general laughter Stephen, knowing that he is losing control of the class, poses his riddle:

> —Tell me now, Stephen said, poking the boy's shoulder with the book, what is a pier.
> —A pier, sir, Armstrong said. A thing out in the waves. A kind of bridge. Kingstown pier, sir.
> Some laughed again: mirthless but with meaning. Two in the back bench whispered. Yes. They knew: had never learned nor ever been innocent. All. With envy he watched their faces. Edith, Ethel, Gerty, Lily. Their likes: their breaths, too, sweetened with tea and jam, their bracelets tittering in the struggle.
> —Kingstown pier, Stephen said. Yes, a disappointed bridge.
> The words troubled their gaze.
> —How, sir? Comyn asked. A bridge is across a river.(*U* 24–25)

The "riddle" and its answer relate to Stephen's own situation, for he identifies himself with the pier as a type of "disappointed bridge." If the bridge symbolizes all forms of communication and intercourse, the disappointment that transforms a bridge into a pier suggests the isolation that leaves Stephen artistically and emotionally frustrated. Furthermore, the passage strongly suggests the inadequacy of Stephen's previous sexual encounters as a substitute for a genuinely personal love. While the phallic pier lies among the waves that are themselves a sexual image (since the tide is related to the menstrual cycle by way of the moon's presumed influence on both), the purely sexual love represented by Kingstown pier and its streetwalkers is ultimately unsatisfying, and Stephen finds himself emotionally isolated.

There are symbolic indications in the riddle that one of the primary causes of Stephen's isolation is the powerful influence of the memory of his mother. Water is a recurrent symbol for woman in Joyce's works, and Stephen associates the sea with his mother and her death (*U* 5, 580). His aversion to bathing in the bay, where Mulligan takes his morning swim, derives in part from this symbolic association. Stephen's constant fear of drowning, similarly, is a metaphor for his fear that family ties and the memory of his mother will "drown" him—hold him fettered and unable to create freely: when he sees his sister Dilly he thinks, "She is drowning. Agenbite. Save her. Agenbite. All against us. She will drown me with her, eyes and hair. Lank coils of seaweed hair around me, my heart, my soul. Salt green death" (*U* 243). This fear of "drowning" relates Stephen's isolation to his dead mother and to the various ties (familial, religious, national) that she at times represents. Moreover, in view of the strongly sexual connotations of the "pier" passage, the representation of Stephen as a pier, and the association of his mother with the surrounding waters, there is a suggestion that Stephen's emotional and artistic frustration derives from an attachment to his mother that has incestuous overtones. Not fully developed here, these implications of incest acquire more meaning in light of Stephen's second riddle.

When the lesson turns to literature—to Milton's *Lycidas* and its image of Christ walking on water (a link with the earlier riddle)—the thought of Christ's "riddling sentence" and the literary theme of the lesson combine to bring to Stephen's mind part of a traditional riddle:

> *Riddle me, riddle me, randy ro.*
> *My father gave me seeds to sow.*

(*U* 26)

Stephen suppresses the rest, but Weldon Thornton has cited a riddle that is either the one Stephen has in mind or a variant on it: "Riddle me, riddle me, randy-bow,/ My father gave me seed to sow,/ The seed was black and the ground was white./ Riddle me that and I'll give you a pipe (variant: pint).—Writing a letter."[3] Thornton's source, Archer Taylor, lists nine riddles of this type; in all but one, the answers involve writing.[4] Taylor notes that "The comparison of writing to strewing black seeds on white land is old and widely known" and that "Adaptations of this manner of description to other themes than writing are rare."[5] Stephen's suppression of the answer and part of the riddle stems partly from the "literary" theme of the riddle: as Thornton observes, Stephen leaves the riddle incomplete "because the riddle and its solution remind him of his failure to justify himself as an author."

There are, however, other reasons for the suppression of the remainder of the riddle. The line *"My father gave me seeds to sow"* implies the theme of passing the "seed" from one generation to the next; this theme is related to the idea that the father and son are "consubstantial" (*U* 38), an idea that Stephen finds troublesome. The image of sowing seeds is sexually suggestive (this is reinforced by the word "randy"), so that in the riddle Stephen's artistic and sexual concerns are symbolically related. Furthermore, the symbolism points toward incest. I have suggested that there are incestous implications in the image of the phallic pier (representative of Stephen) lying among the waves of the sea-mother in the earlier passage. Here incest is more strongly implied in the sowing of seed in the earth-mother.

Stephen's riddle about sowing seeds in the earth recalls the classical myth of Pyrrha and Deucalion; and since Stephen associates himself with Pyrrhus (*U* 24-25), the fact that "Pyrrha" is the feminine equivalent of "Pyrrhus" may reinforce Joyce's apparent adaptation of the theme of this myth to Stephen's situation. Basically, the story is that Pyrrha and Deucalion, the only people left after the great flood, appealed to the goddess Themis to tell them how they might rebuild their race. She told them: "Depart from my temple, loosen the girdles of your garments and throw behind you the bones of your great mother." Solving this riddling oracle, Deucalion observed that "our great mother is the earth, and by her bones I think the oracle means the stones in the body of the earth." They followed directions and from the stones sprang up a race of people.[6] At least figuratively, they impregnated their "mother." Although Joyce does not seem to have alluded to Pyrrha and Deucalion directly in *Ulysses,* the two assume a major role in *Finnegans Wake,*[7] and the themes and images developed in Ovid's story are certainly relevant to Stephen's thoughts at this point. In addition, Roy Arthur Swanson has commented on Joyce's use of the allegory of rocks as men in *Ulysses,* relating this allegory to the Pyrrha-Deucalion myth and suggesting that the allegory may be an extension of "the wordplay of λᾶοσ, the irregular genitive of λᾶασ (rock), and λαόσ (= people, common men)."[8] This commentary provides an essential link in an elaborate allegorical argument through which the Word (letters) becomes Flesh (men): in the sowing riddle, Stephen's letters are allegorized as seeds; the seeds, in turn, parallel the rocks in Ovid's story (Molly's exclamation "O rocks!" meaning "O balls!" reinforces the association between rocks and "seed"); finally, Joyce uses rocks to represent men, most obviously in the "Wandering Rocks" episode.

These associations are strengthened in Stephen's *Parable of the Plums,* in which Anne Kearns and Florence MacCabe sit atop Nelson's pillar (a phallic image parallel to the pier in the earlier riddle), *"peer*ing up at the statue of the one-handled adulterer" and spitting out "plum*stones" (U* 148, italics mine). The plumstones (which are both seeds and stones) relate the parable both to the riddle about sowing seed and to the Pyrrha-Deucalion story, while an elaborate pun on "pier," "peer," and French *pierre* (stone) implies a connection among Stephen's "pier" riddle, the story of Pyrrha sowing stones, and the women who peer at Nelson's pillar and spit out stones. Following a pattern of evading symbols of creativity, Stephen suppresses a riddle about fertile sowing but describes in great detail the infertile sowing of seed-stones on barren pavement. Since his failure as an author—his inability to sow literary "seed"—is related throughout the novel to his inability to free himself from his mother, the Oedipal implications of Stephen's suppression of a riddle that describes writing as sowing seeds in the earth-mother are quite important.

Like his two previous riddles in "Nestor," Stephen's third riddle centers on the mother-son relationship and the effect of the mother and her death on Stephen's life and his creative potential:

> *The cock crew*
> *The sky was blue:*
> *The bells in heaven*
> *Were striking eleven.*
> *Tis time for this poor soul*
> *To go to heaven.*
>
> (*U* 26)

Unable to answer, the students press Stephen for his solution of the riddle: "The fox burying his grandmother under a hollybush." Thornton prints a riddle that is almost identical with Stephen's, but with a significantly different answer: "The fox burying his *mother* under a holly tree" (italics mine). He comments that "If this is the riddle Stephen knows, it is significant, especially since Mulligan has suggested that Stephen killed his mother . . . that he substitutes grandmother for mother as the object of the murder that he assumes took place."9 The two extremes of Stephen's attitude toward his mother, love and hate, are magnified symbolically into incest and murder, and Stephen's alteration of the fox riddle serves to ward off guilt over one extreme as his suppression of the sowing riddle wards off guilt over the other extreme.

Conversely, the substitution of grandmother for mother may be interpreted on the sexual level: digging in the earth, like seed-sowing, is sexually suggestive, and Stephen may attempt to avoid this level of meaning by converting the first object of his infantile love, his mother, into a woman old enough to dispel any implication of sexual attraction. The Oedipal overtones of

Stephen's riddle have also been noted by Alan Dundes, who analyzes the riddle as an allusion to a folktale in which a character named Mr. Fox plans to murder his fiancée but is caught before he can carry out his plan: Dundes notes that in Stephen's riddle "the mother is equivalent to a sweetheart."[10] At the same time, in view of Stephen's fear that he killed, or might be drowned by, his mother, and his apparent identification of himself with Pyrrhus, it is interesting to note that he thinks of Pyrrhus being killed by a "beldam" (*U* 25). "Beldam" now means "old crone," but the word once meant "grandmother." In this sense, Stephen's riddle about the fox burying his grandmother may be seen as the counterpart to his vision of Pyrrhus's death at the hand of a grandmother figure (although overtones of *belle dame* prevent the sexual theme from disappearing even here).

Equally noteworthy is the parallel between the mother-grandmother substitution in Stephen's answer to his riddle and the father-grandfather substitution in Bloom's riddle, *"Brothers and sisters had he none, / Yet that man's father was his grandfather's son"* (*U* 708). Thornton, who cites the usual version of this riddle ("Brothers and sisters have I none, but that man's father is my father's son.—The man is the speaker's own son"), comments that Joyce may have "modified the riddle to fit the situation of the image in the mirror."[11] In view of Stephen's suppression of part of one riddle and his modification of another in order to ward off painful feelings, however, it seems likely that Bloom alters the riddle because the subject of paternity is as distressing to him as the mother-son relationship is to Stephen: not only did Bloom's only son die in infancy, making Bloom a frustrated father, but his own father (for whom his son was named) committed suicide.

Stephen's fox riddle is the starting point for an important motif. Although publicly he changes "mother" to "grandmother," Stephen soon thinks of the riddle in such a way that there can be no doubt that the "poor soul gone to heaven" is his mother and he is the fox with "red reek of rapine in his fur" (*U*

28). Later, when the dog on Sandymount Strand digs in the sand, Stephen relates him to the fox: "Something he buried there, his grandmother" (*U* 46). In "Circe" a chance comment that it is past eleven recalls the riddle, and Stephen recites a slightly garbled version (*U* 558). His answer this time extends the significance of the riddle: "Thirsty fox. . . . Burying his grandmother. Probably he killed her" (*U* 559). The fox is in general a symbol for the cunning quarry that Stephen imagines himself to be (this point is underscored by his fear of dogs); the fox's thirst is another point of comparison between Christ, who thirsted on the cross, and Stephen, who saw a parallel between Christ's "riddling sentence" and his sowing riddle. Elsewhere, Stephen associates himself with Shakespeare, whom he envisions as a "Christfox in leather trews" (*U* 193). The connection of both Stephen and Shakespeare with the fox who buried his grandmother suggests to me a certain amount of ambiguity in Stephen's role-playing, for he apparently associates himself both with Shakespeare/ Hamlet *père* and with Hamnet/ Hamlet *fils;* this in turn increases our awareness of the Oedipal strain in Stephen's character as he is symbolically depicted as both son and husband to Ann Hathaway/ Gertrude. As Schutte has observed, Ann Hathaway psychologically "castrated" Shakespeare, and Stephen "associates May Dedalus with Ann Hathaway" as a temptress who destroys her "lover." [12]

Actually, both Stephen and his mother are destructive in their relationship to one another: Stephen "kills" his mother who, he believes, would have killed his creative spirit. While he tries to deny the bestial element in himself, Stephen is both the cunning fox and the dog that mimics the fox's actions by digging in the sand. There is also a parallel between the fox who digs in the earth and the "greatgrandfather" rat that Bloom sees digging in Glasnevin Cemetery (*U* 114; cf. 118, 474). Bloom thinks of the rat devouring a corpse: "One of those chaps would make short work of a fellow. Pick the bones clean no matter who it was. Ordinary meat for them." These thoughts in turn relate to Stephen's expression of horror and disgust: "Ghoul!

Chewer of corpses!" (*U* 10; cf. 581). On one level the ghoul is the *dio boia* or "hangman god" of wanton destruction (*U* 213); on another level, as Schutte maintains, the ghoul is "Stephen himself, who has just been feeding on his mother's body, which is now decaying";[13] on a third level, the ghoul is Stephen's mother, who he fears would have devoured him (the idea that his mother would have drowned him seems to apply here). The last interpretation—Mrs. Dedalus as potential ghoul—is underscored by her maiden name, May Goulding, which implies a dual role: she is both the youthful, life-giving lover (May suggesting springtime) and the destroyer or "ghoul."[14]

It is no coincidence that *Ulysses,* with all its unsolved, suppressed, or altered riddles, abounds in frustrated relationships: Stephen has lost a mother, Bloom a father and a son; Stephen is alienated from his father, while Bloom has not had sexual intercourse with Molly for "a period of 10 years, 5 months and 18 days" (*U* 736). Although these relationships are to some extent played out in the conscious minds of the characters, their deeper implications seem too painful to be approached directly; hence they are developed through indirect means such as riddles. While it is obvious that Stephen's riddles relate to his attitude toward his mother and her death, it is not so immediately apparent that a symbolic statement about Bloom's relations with Molly is developed through a riddling motif. Yet the *leitmotiv* of *The Rose of Castille,* which is several times expressed as a riddle (first by Lenehan, later by Bloom), provides a complex and urbane commentary on Bloom and the state of his marriage.

Lenehan's *Rose of Castille* riddle, which Bloom later hears and adopts, exemplifies Joyce's use of a riddling motif to describe what the characters will not, perhaps cannot, understand in more direct terms. In the *Dubliners* story "Two Gallants," Lenehan is described as a "sporting vagrant armed with a vast stock of stories, limericks and riddles." His riddle in *Ulysses,* like his limerick and his palindromes, appears at first to be merely another demonstration of a superficial (and probably secondhand) verbal cleverness. The riddle, "What opera resembles a railway line?" (*U* 132, 134), is a conundrum or pun-riddle, as the answer reveals: *"The Rose of Castille.* See the wheeze? Rows of cast steel" (*U* 134). The importance of this riddle in *Ulysses* derives from its symbolic depiction of the unsatisfactory relationship between Bloom and his wife: *The Rose of Castille* is a motif primarily associated with Molly Bloom (an opera singer who was born in Gibraltar, has some Spanish blood, and is often associated in Bloom's mind with the rose), while the "Rows of cast steel," suggesting the railway tracks along which Molly and Boylan will travel on their upcoming concert tour, symbolize the increasing estrangement of Mr. and Mrs. Bloom.[15]

There are many allusions to *The Rose of Castille* in *Ulysses* ("the Rose of Castille" even finds its way into the list of "Irish heroes and heroines of antiquity" in the "Cyclops" episode—*U* 297). In the overture to the "Sirens" chapter there are three allusions to the opera: "A jumping rose on satiny breasts of satin, rose of Castille"; "O rose! . . . Castille"; and "Last rose Castille of summer left bloom I feel so sad alone" (*U* 256-57). The last phrase overlaps allusions to *The Rose of Castille* (associated generally with Molly) and to Thomas Moore's "The Last Rose of Summer," a song motif associated with Bloom, who is the last male in his line and therefore the last Virag-Flower-Bloom (cf. Bloom as the "last sardine of summer," *U* 289). Since Rudy's death (the cause of Bloom's being the last of his line) is partly responsible for Bloom's unsatisfactory relations with Molly, the "Last Rose of Summer" motif refers obliquely to the failure of Bloom's marriage.[16] More obviously, the juxtaposition of the musical motifs associated with Molly and Bloom reflects the marriage that has lost its "bloom," leaving Bloom to "feel so sad alone."

The three statements of the *Rose of Castille* motif in the overture find their parallels in three statements in the "Sirens" episode proper. Lenehan calls Mina Kennedy, one of the barmaids, "rose of Castille" before Bloom enters the Ormond bar (*U* 264), and Bloom later thinks of the same phrase in connection with the other barmaid, Lydia Douce (*U* 286). At the end of the chapter the phrase reappears, referring again to Lydia and uniting the *Rose of Castille* and "Last Rose of Summer" motifs (*U* 290). The point in associating *The Rose of Castille* with these barmaids seems to be that like most of the girls and women Bloom sees, they are surrogates for Molly: Molly herself says that she was "like a rose" (*U* 756) and agrees with Bloom's description of her as a flower, adding that all women are flowers: "yes he said I was a flower of the mountain yes so we are flowers all a womans body yes" (*U* 782).

Up to this point Bloom has not heard Lenehan tell his riddle or refer in any way to *The Rose of Castille,* but during the drinking in Burke's pub toward the end of the "Oxen of the Sun" episode Lenehan repeats his riddle and Bloom apparently hears it above the shouting (*U* 426). In "Circe," when Bloom imagines himself being apprehended by the watch and (as Henry Flower) charged with vagrancy, he tries to pretend that his *nom de plume* is a joke: "You know that old joke, rose of Castille. Bloom. The change of name Virag" (*U* 455). Bloom is referring to the fact that Virag is Hungarian for Flower, but he also seems to be alluding to Juliet's contention that a "rose/ By any other name would smell as sweet."[17] The change of name, however, prefigures a change of sex, for the application of a feminine motif (associated with Molly and other women) to Bloom is one of the earliest indications of the mental sexual reversals that Bloom will undergo in this chapter. Later Bloom, who imagines himself becoming a successful entertainer, tells a rather garbled version of Lenehan's riddle, one that points specifically to Gibraltar, where Molly was born: "What railway opera is like a tramline in Gibraltar? The Rows of Casteele" (*U* 491). The symbolic sexual reversal implied by Bloom's association of himself with *The Rose of Castille* is graphically displayed when, almost immediately after telling the riddle, Bloom is saved from a lynch mob by Dr. Dixon's assertion that "Professor Bloom is a finished example of the new womanly man"; shortly thereafter Bloom expresses his desire to be a mother, and promptly gives birth to eight sons (*U* 493-94). Since the number eight is often associated with Molly, Bloom's octuplets underscore his usurpation of Molly's role—a usurpation that displays, absurdly yet pathetically, Bloom's desperate desire for a son to carry on his name.

Although Lenehan's riddle seems at first to be little more than a play on words, it is the first statement of an important motif that, among other things, illustrates a significant dimension of Bloom's character: the link between his latent femininity and his disappointing relationship with his wife, the Rose of Castille. Bloom's other riddles comment on his situation—the genealogical riddle that he alters reflects his failure as a father, and the conundrum "Where was Moses when the candle went out?" ironically relates Bloom and Moses as bringers of the light who are themselves "in the dark"—but nowhere is Joyce's interweaving of theme and technique more successful than in the complex *Rose of Castille* riddle motif. Symbolically, the metamorphosis of *Rose of Castille* into "Rows of cast steel" in the riddle reflects the metamorphoses of Bloom (into Henry Flower, a mother, etc.) and of the riddle itself (from Lenehan's version into Bloom's), while the strained pun that relates question and answer finds equivalents in a strained marital relationship and in the tension that exists between the male and female poles of Bloom's mind.

The riddles of *Ulysses* are an example of the consistently enigmatic quality of the book itself. Of course, many other puzzles could be cited as well. Who, really, is Martha Clifford? What is meant by the letters "U.P." on the postcard sent to Denis Breen? Who narrates the "Cyclops" chapter? In "Aeolus" alone, we are presented with such teasers as the precise nature of Martin Cunningham's "spellingbee conundrum," the form of the code Ignatius Gallaher used to cable his report on the Phoenix Park murders, and the meaning of Stephen's *Parable of the Plums*. In recent years critics have debated why Molly moves her furniture and whether or not Molly's parents were married, and from time to time there are rumors that a literary sleuth has discovered that *Ulysses* was really a code of some sort. Clearly, though, the book is not simply a code or a cipher, and readers who insist on knowing exactly what is meant by the book's final "Yes," or who M'Intosh is, have missed much of the point of *Ulysses*. Joyce's failure to resolve all the puzzles that he sets up is an indication of his rejection of dogma, of rational certitude, of reductive or simplistic visions of reality. And because it is the nature of the riddle to offer apparent clarity while reserving its irreducible complexities for later examination, the riddle, with its misleading equation of dissimilar objects or words, mocks our confidence in our fallible, incomplete vision of our world and ourselves.

What Joyce developed in one book he used again in the next, refining and modifying techniques in order to correlate them to the overall scheme of his book. In *Finnegans Wake* the riddle is again employed to state problems of identity, to reveal those aspects of relationships that are too painful (often because of incestuous overtones) to approach more directly, and to symbolize the elusive, relative nature of all knowledge. As an elaborate and deliberately misleading metaphor, the "true" riddle is clearly related to the systems of metaphoric correspondences that inform *Ulysses* and *Finnegans Wake,* while the conundrum's reliance on verbal congruity relates this device to the complex wordplay that carries much of the meaning of the *Wake*. The labyrinthine ways of *Finnegans Wake,* which are even more tortuous than those of *Ulysses,* require a technique that reveals yet conceals, that directs the reader toward provisional solutions of the book's mysteries while misleading him, and that forces him to sniff out false trails (they are never completely irrelevant) and to probe beneath the surface for the real concerns of the dreamer. In the riddle, Joyce found a device that fulfilled these paradoxical needs.

3
This Nightly Quisquiquock of the Twelve Apostrophes: The Quiz Chapter of *Finnegans Wake*

Any discussion of Joyce's use of riddles in *Finnegans Wake* must include analyses of specific riddles such as the Prankquean's riddle, Shem's "first riddle of the universe," and Izod's "heliotrope" riddle in The Mime of Mick, Nick and the Maggies. Of all the episodes in the *Wake* that involve riddling questions, none is longer or more complex than the "quiz" chapter, I.6 (126-68), which takes the form of a giant riddle contest—"this nightly quisquiquock of the twelve apostrophes" (126.6-7). The function of this chapter within the narrative framework of *Finnegans Wake,* however, is fairly easy to describe. At the end of an extensive examination of Shem's letter—figuratively, the *Wake* itself—in I.5, the narrator proclaims that there is no need for the Four Old Men (who served as judges in the trial of Festy King in I.4, in which the letter was entered as evidence) to quiz "weekenders" about the *dramatis personae* of the letter—to ask them riddles such as "shoots off in a hiss, muddles up in a mussmass and his wholc's a dismantled noondrunkard's son" (125.1-2).[1] Necessary or not, a series of twelve questions, each centering on a major personage, symbol, or theme, follows in the next chapter. The catechistic technique seems to have been particularly suited to Joyce's temperament, for the technique is employed in the "Nestor" and "Ithaca" chapters of *Ulysses* and again in the Yawn chapter of *Finnegans Wake* (III.3), in which the Four interrogate an exhausted, decomposing Shaun. In I.6 the questions (with one exception) are posed by Shem or "Jockit Mic Ereweak"; eight of the answers are given by "Shaun Mac Irewick," who "left his free natural ripostes to four of them in their own fine artful disorder" (126.4-9).[2] Placed between the analysis of the letter and Shaun's attack on Shem as the author of the letter (I.7), the sixth chapter of the *Wake* not only serves as a link in the narrative thread and develops a great many significant themes (including the all-important conflict between Shem and Shaun), it also reproduces in miniature the structure of the novel. As such, the quiz section provides the reader with a variety of approaches to the riddle of *Finnegans Wake*.

In this chapter I shall be concerned primarily with the first, fourth, and ninth questions and answers: the Finn MacCool riddle (126.10-139.14), the "Irish capitol city" riddle (140.8-141.7), and the "collideorscape" riddle (143.3-28). These three passages illustrate various ways in which Joyce adapts riddles to his thematic and technical concerns in the *Wake:* the first question, the description of the hero, exemplifies the use of cataloguing in motif agglomeration; the fourth question, the description of the setting, illustrates the distortion of narrative perspective and the treatment of one subject (man) in terms of another (city); the ninth question, the description of the dream, is one of the most direct statements of the technical bases of *Finnegans Wake*. To place these passages in their context, however, it is first necessary to obtain a broad view of the structure and themes of the quiz chapter in relation to the rest of *Finnegans Wake*.

The questions begin with a lengthy description of the hero (126.10-139.13). Shaun's answer—"Finn MacCool!"—is partly correct, for many of the details of the riddle describe the Irish hero who was "first of the fenians" (131.9), but on a broader level the proper response would be "Everyman" or "H.C. Earwicker." The second question, "Does your mutter know your mike?" (139.15), may mean "Does your mother [German *Mutter*] know you're St. Michael [one of Shaun's symbolic roles]?" or "Does your speech [muttering] have any relationship to the voice box [microphone] that produces it?" The latter interpretation is important because it involves the question whether any phenomenon "knows" the agent that produced it (cf. Stephen Dedalus's musings on the father-son relationship in *Ulysses*), but in his answer Shaun chooses to elaborate on the relationship between his parents. His response, part of which echoes the rhythm of Father Prout's "The Bells of Shandon," describes a "dirty . . . purty . . . flirty" woman who gives her husband erections and causes his wet dreams—or, alternately, arouses him and then urinates on him in a recapitulation of the Prankquean's conquest of Jarl van Hoother (21-23). The emphasis falls on the woman's role as the temptress whose "pranklings" would cause any man, from "hot Hammurabi" to "cowld Clesiastes," to go astray.

The third question (139.29-140.5) asks for the "true-to-type motto-in-lieu" for Earwicker's pub. The answer, "Thine obesity, O civilian, hits the felicitude of our orb!" parodies Dublin's city motto, *Obedientia civium urbis felicitas* ("The obedience of the citizens is the happiness of the town"), a phrase that appears throughout the *Wake*. Significantly, Shaun's answer reveals not his father's obedience but his obesity, a sign of the decadence that will leave the older man vulnerable to attack from the younger generation. The next question, which shifts us from the pub to the nearby metropolis, asks what "Irish capitol city . . . of two syllables and six letters, with a deltic origin [beginning with D] and a nuinous end [ending with N]" has the largest public park in the world (Phoenix Park—cf. 564.11-12), the most expensive brewery (Guinness's),[3] the widest public thoroughfare (O'Connell Street),[4] and "the most phillohippuc theobibbous paùpulation in the world" (the world's most impoverished population of horse-loving communicants). The obvious answer is Dublin, but the Four Old Men, representing the four Irish provinces, answer the question, and each insists that the "capital" of his province (Belfast in Ulster, Cork in Munster, Dublin in Leinster, Galway in Connacht) is the correct response. The fifth question and its answer (141.8-27) identify "Pore ole Joe," an elderly version of Earwicker, as the person who cleans up the pub and performs odd jobs. The sixth question is fairly direct: "What means the saloon slogan Summon In The Housesweep Dinah?" (141.28-29). The question echoes lines from the chorus of "I've Been Working on the Railroad" that appear in *Ulysses* in the context of sexual infidelity (*U* 443). The answer by Kate the cleaning woman, an elderly version of Anna Livia, begins with complaints about the amount of work heaped upon her and references to her knowledge of Earwicker's sin ("I thawght I knew his stain on the flower") and to her younger days when "he called [me] by me midden name"; concluding with contemptuous annoyance, she demands to know "who bruk the dandleass and who seen the blackcullen jam," she expresses hope that tomorrow's picnic will be spoiled by rain, and she offers us a plateful of *"Shite!"*

The seventh question (142.8-28) lists the occupations, addresses, and names of the twelve customers in Earwicker's pub. They are identified as the "Morphios"—Murphys under the influence of Morpheus. The next question, "And how war yore maggies?" (142.30), introduces the eternal theme of the battle of the sexes. The ninth question, one of the most important passages in the book, describes the dream situation and asks for a definition of what the dreamer envisions (143.3-27). Shaun's answer is "A collideorscape!"—not a bad description of *Finnegans Wake*. The tenth question, which centers on the nature of love, is answered appropriately enough by Issy, Earwicker's daughter, who knows more about the subject than either of her brothers (143.29-148.32).

The introduction of the sister prepares the reader for the battle of the brothers. In the eleventh question Shem asks, in essence, whether Shaun would under any circumstances come to the aid of his poor, exiled, blind brother. The conclusion of the question, however, indicates that Shem expects a refusal:

"we don't think, Jones, we'd care to this evening, would you?" (149.9-10). True to form, Shaun denies Shem ("No, blank ye!"), but he feels compelled to explain his rejection of his brother through a lengthy lecture which includes an attack on time-oriented people such as Bergson, Einstein, and Shem (149.11-152.3); The Fable of the Mookse and the Gripes, with Shaun (the Mookse) as Pope Adrian IV and Shem (the Gripes) as Ireland (152.15-159.18); another analysis of the "dime-cash" or time-space problem (159.24-161.14); and the story of Burrus, Caseous, and Margareen (161.15-167.17). Ignoring (or ignorant of) the inconclusiveness of his *exempla,* Shaun completes his lecture with yet another detailed rejection of Shem (167.18-168.12). The twelfth and last question and answer, however, hint at the eventual reunion of the twins. Phrased as an imperative but punctuated as a question, Shaun's *"Sacer esto?"* expresses perfectly the complex moral vision of the *Wake:* Shaun's command is both a curse and a blessing, and his question is not only whether his brother will be accursed but also whether he will be blessed (both meanings are implicit in Latin *sacer*). Shem's answer, *"Semus sumus!",* is, as Tindall observes, "both singular and plural" and "means I am Shem and we are the same."[5]

The structure of the quiz chapter is more coherent than this summary indicates; actually the chapter, like the book, is cyclical, and the questions are grouped into clearly defined stages which parallel Giambattista Vico's division of each cycle of history into three major ages (divine, heroic, and human or civil) and the *ricorso* or transitional period between cycles.[6] The twelve questions, then, may be divided into three "ages" of four questions each. The following analysis, based on a similar study by Clive Hart and Fritz Senn,[7] illustrates some of the correspondences between the Viconian pattern and the structure of the sixth chapter.

Questions 1, 5, and 9 center on Earwicker, who is first the young, virile Finn MacCool, then "Pore ole Joe," and finally the dreamer whose kaleidoscopic vision of past, present, and future is described in the "collideorscape" riddle.[8] Questions 2, 6, and 10 show us Anna Livia as mother, old woman, and young temptress. The relationship that exists among questions 3, 7, and 11, the third question in each of the subcycles, is less obvious, but apparently these questions represent Earwicker's creations (the pub and the city whose motto it bears in question 3; the pub, again, where the Morphios convene nightly, in question 7; the sons in question 11). Creation brings the Fall, as the hod carrier Tim Finnegan learned, and in the last question in each minor cycle (4, 8, and 12) there are both the confusion and the promise of renewal that characterize the *ricorso* between Viconian cycles. Hence what appears to be a relatively simple question about Dublin is confused through the provincial loyalties of the Four, but, as Campbell and Robinson note, the responses finally "melt together and are harmonized in the lilting tonalities of the bells of Shandon."[9] The warring of the maggies in question 8 brings confusion until leap year ("elope year") when Issy "picks one man more" and begins the next cycle. In the final question the ambiguity of *sacer* as blessing and curse parallels the ubiquitous *O felix culpa!* theme, and the union of the brothers *("Semus sumus!")* promises renewal.

The twelve questions actually involve one relatively coherent cyclical action, the pattern often being invoked through allusion rather than by direct statement. This pattern is, I believe, easiest to follow when we begin with the "collideorscape" riddle (question 9). Here an aging, weary man is dreaming about the materials of the *Wake*. Lingering momentarily between death and rebirth (the *ricorso*), he sees all of history in one "futule preteriting unstant." The other eleven questions form a cycle that reproduces the pattern of the dream and returns us to the dreamer. In question 10 Issy begins the cycle by teasing her brothers and provoking the conflict that breaks out in the eleventh question and answer. In this section Issy, as Nuvoletta (157.8), is unable to reconcile the Mookse and the Gripes, who are eventually carried off by two women and replaced by "an only elmtree and but a stone" (159.4).[10] In the story of Burrus

and Caseous the boys remain divided: Margareen (Issy) sees B
and C as the base of an "isocelating biangle" and piles hatboxes
on them in order to reach A ("Antonius, a wop") at the top of
the triangle (165.8–167.8). Antonius represents the union of
Burrus and Caseous (167.1–3), but union is postponed while
Shaun returns to his attack on Shem.[11] In the twelfth question,
however, Shaun unwittingly gives Shem an opportunity to
declare the union of the twins *("Semus sumus!");* united, they
become Finn MacCool in a cyclic return to the first question.

Having passed through a period comparable to Vico's divine
age (the period of birth and childhood), Shem and Shaun are
now united in one figure in Vico's heroic age, a period characterized by the institution of matrimony. Finn MacCool, the
heroic aspect of the new H.C. Earwicker (question 1), marries
Anna Livia Plurabelle, a more mature version of Issy (question
2), and builds a city—Dublin—or at least a pub bearing the
city's motto (question 3). This phase represents the hero at the
height of his powers, but the appearance of the Four Old Men
as representatives of the Irish provinces in the fourth question
signals the end of a cycle, as it does in I.4 (the Four passing
judgment on Festy King), in II.4 (the Four spying on Tristan
and Iseult), and in III.4 (the Four viewing Mr. and Mrs. Porter
in bed). In the fifth question Earwicker is himself an old man
(Joe), and in the sixth question the young, desirable mother-
temptress, Anna Livia, is transformed into shrewish, aging
Kate. This third cycle is Vico's civil or human age, characterized
by old age and death; hence the Morphios in question 7 are not
only the customers in Earwicker's pub and the jury that will try
him, they are also the twelve mourners at his wake. The allusion
to Morpheus prefigures the description of the sleeping/dying
dreamer of question 9; first, however, the temptresses make
their appearance in the form of the maggies (question 8). These
girls—like Issy and her mirror image, the two girls in the Park,
and the seven rainbow girls—are a multiple version of Issy; they
should be identified with the twenty-eight girls from St. Bride's
Academy in III.2. Issy, the leap-year girl, emerges as the

twenty-ninth, and she is preparing to pick her man as her father begins his dream (question 9).

Finn MacCool!

The Finn MacCool riddle (question 1), which consists of nearly four hundred attributes of Finn-Earwicker, is the most extensive catalogue in *Finnegans Wake*. Joyce liked comic catalogues and used them frequently in his novels. In *A Portrait of the Artist as a Young Man* Stephen enumerates his father's "occupations" in comic fashion (*P* 241), and in *Ulysses* there are many such catalogues, including the list of "Irish heroes and heroines of antiquity" whose "tribal images" are engraved on seastones which hang from the Cyclops's belt (*U* 296-97); the list of those who join in the mock-pursuit of Bloom as he leaves Bella Cohen's (*U* 586-87); and the list of Molly's "lovers" (*U* 731). The elements of fantasy and exaggeration in these lists are typical of most of the catalogues in *Ulysses,* and these elements are even more prominent in the *Wake* catalogues. In *Finnegans Wake* Joyce presents us with catalogues of the abusive names that a drunken American called Earwicker (71.10-72.16); proposed titles for Anna Livia's letter (104.5-107.7); the occupations, addresses, and first names of the Morphios (142.8-28); Shem's physical attributes (169.11-20); games the children once played (176.1-18); the contents of Shem's house (183.8-184.4); Anna Livia's gifts for her children (210.6-212.17); the children's theme topics (306.13-308.1); and the qualities of Earwicker's home and family (543.22-545.14). Smaller catalogues appear and reappear; lists of seven (seven girls, seven articles of clothing, seven colors of the rainbow, seven deadly sins, Earwicker's seven wives, the seven wonders of the ancient world) are particularly important.

As parodies of the epic catalogue, the longer catalogues in *Finnegans Wake* serve a dual function: they establish a parallel (one of many) between the *Wake* and the epic, and at the same time they underscore the differences between the portrayal of humanity in a heroic poem and the dreamer's awareness of both the heroic and the distinctly nonheroic qualities of Joyce's middle-class hero. Bernard Benstock, moreover, has noted that the catalogues repeat "basic themes in succinct form" and parody "contemporary song titles, slogans, epithets, and clichés and key words which are bandied about every day until they lose their significance and become mere catch phrases."[12] Most importantly, the catalogues serve as motivistic rubbish-heaps (paralleling the dump in which Biddy the Hen found the letter); as such, they are convenient places for lumping together motifs, both external (allusive) and internal (nonallusive). A comparison of the version of the Finn MacCool riddle printed in Hayman's edition of the early drafts with the final version shows that the catalogue grew from approximately one page in 1926 or 1927 to thirteen pages in 1939; as the plan for the book became more concrete, Joyce collected motifs associated with the hero and added them to his catalogue in progress.[13] Since Earwicker's qualities are "variously catalogued, regularly regrouped" (129.12), the order in which the motifs appear in the catalogue is of little importance and, as Hart has observed, is usually completely arbitrary: Joyce seems to have wanted "to create a series of nodal points where the reader can contemplate the primary materials at his leisure; the essence of the book is refined off from the more impure discursive matter and is shown forth for a moment before the cycles begin again."[14]

During the composition of I.6 Joyce used a series of symbols to represent the first eleven questions: ⊓ (1); △ (2); □ (3); × (4); ⋚ (5); κ (6); ○ (7); ⌒ (8); ⊕ (9); ⊣ (10); ⋀ (11).[15] Six of these symbols appear together elsewhere in *Finnegans Wake* (299.F4), and some explanation of these symbols and one of the others is provided by Joyce's letter to Harriet Shaw Weaver (24 March 1924).[16] In another letter three years later Joyce explained that the symbol ⊔ is a Chinese pictograph for "mountain" and shortly thereafter he wrote to Miss Weaver that ⊔ "means H C E interred in the landscape."[17] Dead, Earwicker becomes a mountain—or Tim Finnegan stretched out at his wake (6.32). By rotating the symbol counterclockwise we can follow Earwicker's resurrection and his progression through the ages of a Viconian cycle:

> ... ⊒ signifies HCE's resurrection, ⊓ his presence in prehistoric form (Stonehenge), and E his existence as Earwicker, the Everyman of modern times. Thus ⊒ , ⊓ , E , and ⊔ represent the four-part Viconian cycle (Resurrection, Heroic accomplishment, Civil extension, and the Fall) which is the major structural principle of the *Wake*.[18]

Accordingly, the use of the symbol ⊓ for the Finn MacCool riddle implies that the person described in the riddle is one (or all) of the many heroic aspects of HCE. In his heroic phase Earwicker is most often incarnated as Finn MacCool, the father of Ossian and the greatest hero in the Fenian or Ossianic cycle of Irish myths; among other things the symbol ⊓ may be intended to represent the letter M for MacCool. Beechhold has listed a score of phrases in the riddle that "are reminiscent of various details of the Fenian material, especially of Finn as he is drawn in the old tales,"[19] and even this list hardly exhausts the Fenian allusions in the riddle. For instance, although the "hunt for the boar trwth" (132.4-5) refers primarily to the Arthurian legend of "The Wooing of Olwen," in which a boar is named Truith or Trwyth, it may also allude to the boar hunt in which Dermot, Finn's younger rival for Grania's love, was killed. Another allusion that does not appear in Beechhold's list is "was drummatoysed by Mac Milligan's daughter" (133.26), which Atherton cites as a reference to Alice Milligan's one-act play *The Last Feast of the Fianna*.[20] The action of the play occurs after Dermot's death and Finn's subsequent marriage to Grania; a woman of the Sidhe, Niamh, appears at Finn's door and, being admitted despite Grania's objections, entices away Finn's son Ossian. Interestingly enough, Finn's comment in the play that his door, "at feasting time, was never shut on any guest," combined with the theme of the abduction of the son, establishes a connection between the material of Alice Milligan's Celtic Twilight drama and the quasi-historical account of the visit of the piratess Grace O'Malley (Gráinne Ni Mhaille in Irish) at the castle of the Earl of Howth. This story, which Joyce uses as the core story for The Tale of Jarl van Hoother and the Prankquean, involves the Earl's refusal to open his castle doors to the uninvited guest who arrives at dinnertime, the retaliatory kidnaping of the Earl's son, and the extortion from the Earl of a promise that his doors would always be open at mealtime. In the riddle the phrase "eats with doors open" (129.19-20) refers primarily to the Earl's promise, but it also alludes to Finn's custom of admitting any guest who arrives at mealtime. These connections between the Fenian story which Alice Milligan "drummatoysed" and the Grace O'Malley story strengthen Joyce's interweaving of the Finn-Dermont-Grania theme with the plot outline of the story of Grace O'Malley and the Earl of Howth in the Prankquean episode.

As befits the universal character of HCE or "Here Comes Everybody" (32.18-19), however, the hero described in the riddle is not merely Finn MacCool, although there are more references to Finn than to any other person. For example, the subject of the riddle is also Brian Boru, the Irish high king or *ard ri* ("ardree," 133.36) who drove the Danes from Ireland in the battle of Clontarf in 1014: "indanified himself with boro tribute and was schenkt publicly to brigstoll" (133.28-29). This phrase refers to several related themes: the conflict between the native Irish and varous invaders, the intermarriage and merging of the two groups ("indanified"), and the conquest of the new group by a third force. The last of these themes is incorporated in the phrase "was schenkt publicly to brigstoll," an allusion to Henry II's gift (German *schenkt,* "gives") of the city of Dublin to the people of Bristol ("brigstoll"), England, in 1173. In his role as Dubliner, Earwicker is the victim of this event and his land is stolen while he is thrown in the brig ("brigstoll" again); in his role as British imperialist, however, Earwicker is the oppressor, and in III.3 he plays the part of Henry and gives his property to the people of "Tolbris" (545.14-23).[21] On another level this property is Earwicker's pub, which is alluded to both in "publicly" and in "schenkt" (German *Schenke,* "pub"). Furthermore, as Tindall has observed, there is an allusion to the name of the pub in "brigstoll," since the two names most frequently given to the pub are "Bristol (from bridge) and Mullingar." Tindall comments that "The Mullingar and the Bridge Inn, across the bridge at Chapelizod, are still there. . . . Maybe H.C.E.'s pub, like H.C.E. himself, is dual, half on one bank of the Liffey, half on the other."[22] In view of the association of Bristol with British imperialism, it seems likely that the alternation between the two names for the pub, the Bristol and the "Mullingar Inn" (138.19-20), also symbolizes Earwicker's dual role as imperialist-invader and as native Irishman.

Throughout *Finnegans Wake* references to a white hat or cap allude to the etymology of Finn's name: *fionn cumhal* is "white cap" in medieval Irish, "fair (white) hood" in modern Irish.[23] It is difficult to say how many other "white" references allude to Finn, except in those cases in which the Fenian content is fairly clear: for instance, the juxtaposition of "a saumon taken with a lance" and "a whyterobe lifting a host" (139.3-4) implies a reference to Finn since, according to the widely known story, he gained his wisdom by eating the salmon of knowledge (cf. 132.35). While the white hat identifies a mythical Irish hero, however, the "white horse" (which often overlaps into "wide arse") belongs to the Anglo-Irish hero of Waterloo, the Duke of Wellington. The source of this allusion, which Joyce plays with in the "Willingdone Museyrooom" episode (8.9-10.23), is the story of the young girl who, while touring a wax museum, was told "This is the Duke of Wellington and his horse," and replied "Which is the Duke and which is the horse?" Wellington's white horse appears several times in the Finn MacCool riddle: "had sevenal successivecoloured serebanmaids on the same big white drawringroam horthrug" (126.19-20); "his great wide cloak [cf. Finn's white cap or hood] lies on fifteen acres and his little white horse decks by dozens our doors" (135.21-22); "theer's his bow and wheer's his leaker and heer lays his bequiet hearse, decp" (137.5-7).[24]

One of the allusions to Wellington's white horse is particularly interesting: "his threefaced stonehead was found on a whitehorse hill and the print of his costellous feet is seen in the goat's grasscircle" (132.12-14). This phrase brings us back to the fallen giant Finnegan whose outline appears early in *Finnegans Wake:*

> The great fall of the offwall entailed at such short notice the pftjschute of Finnegan, erse solid man, that the humptyhillhead of humself prumptly sends an unquiring one well to the west in quest of his tumptytumtoes: and their upturnpikepointandplace is at the knock out in the park where oranges have been laid to rust upon the green since devlinsfirst loved livvy. (3.18-24)

Significantly, the "stonehead" lying on a "whitehorse hill" complements the "Wellingtonia Sequoia" (126.12): Earwicker-Wellington is both tree and stone, the symbols for the two poles of his mind that are associated with his two sons. In the Finn MacCool riddle the tree and stone are held together in an uneasy equilibrium: "to all his foretellers he reared a stone and for all his comethers he planted a tree" (135.4-5). In *Finnegans Wake* the Fall splits the aging Earwicker, who in his younger days played the role of Tristan (a unified tree-stone), into the tree and stone: "he crashed in the hollow of the park, trees down, as he soared in the vaguum of the phoenix, stones up" (136.33-35).

The Fall is one of the most important motifs in the catalogue of the attributes of Finn-Earwicker. Since Earwicker's roles are often reversed—"hounded become haunter, hunter become fox" (132.16-17)—the hero is both Jehovah, who "threatens thunder upon malefactors" (127.16), and Adam, weighed down by guilt, who "thought he weighed a new ton when there felled his first lapapple" (126.16-17). (The latter phrase ingeniously confuses Adam's fall through eating the apple with the fall of the apple which, according to popular tradition, inspired Newton's theory of the effect of gravity on falling bodies.) The riddle describes men who are about to fall, like proud Thomas à Becket, another victim of Henry II ("independent of the lordship of chamberlain, acknowledging the rule of Rome," 129.24-26), and men who have fallen, like the mutilated soldier in the Irish song "Och Johnny I Hardly Knew Ye" ("the same homoheatherous checkinlossegg as when sollyeye airly blew ye," 129.14-15). Earwicker's split into two parts after the Fall is compared to the partition of Ireland after 1922 ("partitioned Irskaholm") but his reunification, and perhaps Ireland's too, is foretold by way of allusion to Wolfe Tone's "united Irishmen" (132.33-34). In accord with the Viconian pattern of cyclic renewal, Earwicker "moves in vicous cicles yet remews the same" (134.16-17).

Applied to H.C. Earwicker, the story of the Fall is most often represented as the vaguely defined incident in Dublin's Phoenix Park involving Earwicker, two girls, and three soldiers. Apparently Earwicker defecated or urinated in the Park and was seen and perhaps ridiculed by the girls; or the soldiers caught him spying on the girls, who were urinating; or he was seen masturbating. In any case, references to "two and three" invariably allude to the girls and soldiers who participated in the escapade. Such allusions are abundant, as the following list of references in the Finn MacCool riddle indicates:

> . . . was evacuated at the mere appearance of three germhuns and twice besieged by a sweep (127.12-13) . . . two remarkable piscines and three wellworthseeing ambries (127.35-36) . . . shot two queans and shook three caskles when he won his game of dwarfs (128.17-18) . . . two psychic espousals and three desertions (129.3) . . . shows he's fly to both demisfairs but thries to cover up his tracers (129.21-22) . . . had two cardinal ventures and three capitol sinks (131.1-2) . . . cumbrum, cumbrum, twiniceynurseys fore a drum but tre to uno tips the scale (134.8-9) . . . his rainfall is a couple of kneehighs while his meanst grass temperature marked three in the shade (134.30-32) . . . he hestens towards dames troth and wedding hand like the prince of Orange and Nassau while he has trinity left behind him (135.11-13) . . . a pair of pectorals and a triplescreen to get a wind up (137.26-27).[25]

The two girls in the Park are actually Earwicker's daughter Issy and her mirror image; when they appear as the raven and the dove (136.13, 136.29-30) they are equated with the "jinnies" who plague "Willingdone" (8.33-34). The story of Willingdone, the two jinnies, and the "three lipoleums" (8.30) is of course one of the many versions of the Earwicker-two girls-three soldiers story.

The incestuous implications of Earwicker's sexual encounter with a dual version of his daughter—with his two sons, now expanded to three to give the number of Noah's sons, watching—are obvious enough: Earwicker's guilt, we discover, stems from an inverted "eatupus complex" (128.36). Because the dreamer, who identifies himself with Earwicker, refuses to accept these incestuous impulses, his unconscious mind disguises incest in various ways, but the disguises are never wholly successful. Incest in *Finnegans Wake* is often related to the "insect" motif (29.30, 306.30, 339.22, 414.27), and Earwicker's name, punning on "earwig," reveals his "insectuous" nature. Translated into French, earwig becomes *perce-oreille,* which is Gaelicised into "Persse O'Reilly," the name Earwicker bears in Hosty's satirical ballad which celebrates Earwicker's fall (44-47). In the Finn MacCool riddle the hero who "crawls with lice" and "swarms with saggarts" (135.36) is also Persse O'Reilly, "sponser to a squad of piercers, ally to a host of rawlies" (133.10-11). Teased by his tempting "leapyourown taughter" or leap-year daughter, Issy, Earwicker "is too funny for a fish and has too much outside for an insect" (127.2-3). If the symbol ⊓ which Joyce assigned to the Finn MacCool passage signifies Earwicker in his heroic incarnation, it also, paradoxically, represents him as a crawling insect.

While at one end of the chain of being Earwicker is an insect, at the other end he is not only the human race but the entire universe (at least the male half) and the god who created it. Like the universe of modern physics, Earwicker shrinks and expands (130.26-27, 138.35-36) in another version of the death and resurrection of the hero-god. A succinct description of the process of creation reveals his initials: "heavengendered, chaosfoedted, earthborn" (137.14). Earwicker embodies all creators, not only the poet-builder ("myther rector," 126.10) and father ("a farfar and morefar and a hoar father," 139.5–6) but even the Trinity itself: "the flawhoolagh, the grasping one, the kindler of paschal fire" (128.33–34). Finally, since Earwicker is frequently called Mr. Porter (especially in III.4), he is identified with the porter that he serves in his tavern: "as it gan in the biguinnengs [beginning/Guinness] so wound up in a battle of Boss" (129.10–11). The puns on "In the beginning" (Genesis 1:1, John 1:1) and "As it was in the beginning is now and ever shall be . . . " establish Earwicker-Porter-porter's ale as a sacramental symbol for the creative Word, and this identification is strengthened by the exchange of "a" (alpha = beginning) and "o" (omega = end) in "a bottle of Bass" (Bass's ale) to produce "a battle of Boss." As in *Finnegans Wake* the flesh is made word ("flesch nuemaid motts," 138.8), so in the god-hero-man HCE the Word is made flesh, and Joyce's hero is a microcosm of the circular universe he inhabits.

The "beginning and end" idea manifests itself not only in the hero who is both Alpha and Omega, but also in the structure of the Finn MacCool riddle. As I observed earlier, the order in which the motifs appear in the catalogue seems in general to be arbitrary, but Joyce's preoccupation with parallels and contrasts between the beginnings and ends of all his works (which reaches its zenith in the simultaneous beginning and end of *Finnegans Wake*) suggests that the reader would do well to look for such correspondences at the extremes of the catalogue-riddle. A quick check with Hayman's *First-Draft Version*[26] shows that Joyce determined very early how he wanted to commence and conclude his riddle: virtually all the additions which swelled the catalogue to many times its original size were added to the amorphous center (127–38), while a total of about twelve lines at the two extremes (126.10–16, 139.8–13), which in the final draft account for only 2.5 percent of the lines in the riddle, may be found in essentially the same form in the early drafts, where they account for nearly half the lines. The basic contrast developed between the extremes of the riddle shows man rising and falling, building a structure (like Halvard

Solness and Tim Finnegan) and plummeting from the top. Jack climbs the beanstalk ("the first to rise taller through his beanstale," 126.11) but must eventually descend; Finnegan, the drunken hodcarrier in the song that gave Joyce the title for his book, falls off the scaffolding and is laid out for the wake "With a gallon of whiskey at his feet/ And a barrel of porter at his head" (cf. 139.8-9, "blows whiskery around his summit but stehts stout upon his footles"). Building—one of many forms of creation—always carries sexual implications in the *Wake,* and the "erection" of the builder or "myther rector" is not only a wall, a tower, or a mythical construct, but also a sexual erection that leads to the seduction of the young river-woman Anna Livia: "went nudiboots with trouters into a liffeyette when she was barely in her tricklies" (126.13-14). In contrast, the young seducer becomes, near the end of the riddle, an aging parent or grandparent: "a farfar and morefar and a hoar father Nakedbucker in villas old as new" (139.5-7). The tower (French *phare,* Italian *faro,* "lighthouse") which the builder erects is also the penis of the father (Danish *far*), and both erections lead to a fall.[27] Death follows life as the night the morning—"is Timb to the pearly morn and Tomb to the mourning night" (139.10-11)—but the wake at the end of the riddle (139.10) implies not only death but resurrection or awakening.

Delfas, Dorhqk, Nublid, Dalway

While the Finn MacCool riddle is a complex question with a specific answer, the "Irish capitol city" riddle (140.8-141.7) seems to be a relatively simple question with a complex answer. The symbol Joyce assigned to this question is ×, the sign usually associated with the Four. These garrulous, lecherous, nosy old men surround Shaun, who often stands, sits, or lies (in both senses) at the center of the quincunx.[28] In this passage, the Four respond to Shem's riddle instead of Shaun, although it could be argued that the old men are speaking through Shaun much as Earwicker speaks through Yawn (or Shaun) in III.3. In

1932 Joyce sent the second answer to the riddle to Ezra Pound and noted that "it is the second of the four masters, who here represents Munster, answering."[29] Directed by their provincial viewpoints, the Four view the question in different ways and respond accordingly.

The confusion over the answer to the riddle—an answer that seems so obvious that one must stretch definitions to their limits to call the question a "riddle"—reflects and at the same time parodies Joyce's concern with the search for absolutes in a relativistic universe. If riddling questions are rarely answered correctly in Joyce's works, it is because knowledge is elusive and absolute knowledge is delusive, a point which Joyce repeatedly asserts: "Thus the unfacts, did we possess them, are too imprecisely few to warrant our certitude" (57.16-17). The Four Old Men are the four dimensions of the *Wake*-world (Johnny MacDougall, like Shem, represents time while the synoptic gospelers represent the three dimensions of space), and each views reality, or at least part of it, from a different perspective, "facing one way to another way and this way on that way, from severalled their fourdimmansions" (367.26-27). Inevitably, as Hart observes, their search for an absolute fails:

> Because of this constant mobility of forms and times the search for an absolute is in everybody's mind throughout the book and is the special concern of the ubiquitous Old Men who are involved in trying to find a common denominator for their four different points of view; but the only absolute they ever discover is the absolute uncertainty from which they began, the wholly relative nature of all the cycles.[30]

Quarreling among themselves in traditional Irish fashion, the Four make and break alliances with each other. I.R.A. members Luke, John, and Mark—"leinconnmuns" (521.28) or Leinster, Connacht, and Munster—sometimes attack Matthew (Ulster), playing out the history of partitioned Ireland; at other times one of these allies, usually John, may be the underdog. In the riddle, the questioner—Shem—seems to be associated in some way with Luke or Leinster, the only province with which

This Nightly Quisquiquock of the Twelve Apostrophes 65

Shem, like Joyce, has any clear affinity: the parenthetical exclamations "a dea o dea!" and "ah dust oh dust!" echo Luke Tarpey's characteristic sigh of "ah dear oh dear" and link Shem to the representative of Dublin, the city which (as noted earlier) is the presumptive answer to the riddle. The confusion over the answer, resulting in part from the provincial loyalties of the Four, reflects the confusion that always attends the *ricorso*, the point where beginning and end (alpha and omega—"*a* dea *o* dea") merge in a Viconian cycle. In accordance with Joyce's principle that the movement in the *ricorso* stage is backward, the first and last letters of Dublin are reversed, ironically making "Nublid" the only one of the four Irish capitals named in the answers ("Delfas" for Belfast, "Dorhqk" for Cork, "Nublid" for Dublin, and "Dalway" for Galway) that lacks the "deltic origin" specified in the question.

The five answers—one by each of the Four and a final chorus which harmonizes their "abecedeed responses"—form, as Mrs. Glasheen observes, a courtship poem addressed to Issy, similar to the song they address to Iseult at the end of II.4 (398.31-399.28)[31] Each of the Old Men points out to Issy the advantages of living in his province. Matt Gregory of "Delfas" paints a mock-romantic picture of industrial Ulster: he foresees "the gould hommers of my heart . . . bingbanging again the ribs of yer resistance and the tenderbolts of my rivets working to your destraction" (140.15-18). The gold hammers of Matt's Belfast give way to Mark Lyons's "silvry speech" (140.27), Luke Tarpey's "copper's panful of sybeans" (140.31), and Johnny MacDougall's "Rodiron" (141.3) as the four main parts of the answer correspond to the gold, silver, copper, and iron ages of history. Mark of "Dorhqk" tempts Issy with softer sounds than Matt's industrial noises ("such good old chimes . . . my plovery soft accents") while Luke of "Nublid" invites her to share with him a quiet country life in Dublin, Georgia, where she will concentrate on self-improvement by "churning over the new-leaved butter . . . the choicest and the cheapest from Atlanta to Oconee" while he sleeps in the garden. At this point the confusion between Dublin, Georgia, and Dublin, Ireland, seems to indicate that Shaun, rather than Shem, has the upper hand: the twins meet in Ireland and Australia, the two lands in which Shaun's east-west orbit around the world and Shem's north-south orbit intersect, but never in the United States, to which Shaun alone travels.[32] This, of course, adds an ironic note to Shem's affinity with Luke and Dublin (reflected in the "ah dear oh dear" motif): although Shem undergoes periodic exiles from Dublin, conforming to the pattern set by Joyce himself, the city at this point reverses the process of exile by migrating to America and leaving Shem stranded.

The fourth answer to the riddle comes from John of "Dalway," who speaks in doggerel verse of various places in Connacht ("Mayo I make, Tuam I take, Sligo's sleek but Galway's grace"). The primary motif in this answer is fishing: various fish (eel, salmon, chub, dace) are named, and words such as "hooked," "trotty" (incorporating "trot" or trotline as well as trout), and "Rodiron" develop the fishing motif further. The fish is of course a traditional symbol for Christ, and in the *Wake* this symbol is confused with Finn's salmon of wisdom. In any case the fish represents the forces of life (although it may at the same time be a symbol of death, when Joyce plays French *poisson*, "fish," against English "poison"—cf. 451.6). The fish here apparently represents Earwicker, whose body, like Christ's, is a sacramental meal; references in other parts of the *Wake* connect the hero to the eel, the salmon, and other aquatic creatures,[33] and in the fourth answer he is undoubtedly the "Holy eel and Sainted Salmon, chucking chub and ducking dace," fish for the Friday wake meal.

In the final chorus the Four speak together. Set off as verse, the lines would look like this:

> A bell a bell on Shalldoll Steepbell,
> ond be'll go massplon pristmoss speople,
> Shand praise gon ness our fayst moan *neople*,
>   our prame *Shandeepen*,
>   pay name muy *feepence*,
> moy nay non *Aequallllllll*!

This Nightly Quisquiquock of the Twelve Apostrophes 67

These lines form a loose parody of the style and content of "The Bells of Shandon" by Francis S. Mahony ("Father Prout"). Campbell and Robinson, commenting on this passage, observe that

> in reply to Question 2 the bells of Shandon were associated with Anna Livia. She it is who subsumes all differentiations and recompounds them, their contrarieties eliminated, into one great somebody. Then again it will be she as "Bringer of Plurabilities," who sends all forth again, in forms apparently new.[34]

This comment is a great deal more meaningful than it at first appears. Far from being merely a confusing parody of a poem which is itself a parody, the fifth answer to the riddle is a *sandhi,* the equivalent of the *ricorso* in Indian and theosophical cycles of history which contain four major ages (as opposed to the three ages of a Viconian cycle).[35] At the beginning of Book IV the announcement of the *sandhi* is combined with the ringing of church bells on Sunday morning and with the "Sanctus! Sanctus! Sanctus!" motif: "Sandhyas! Sandhyas! Sandhyas!" (593.1). Similarly, the bells of Shandon seem here to promise renewal. The first four answers, as I have observed, correspond to the fourfold series of world-ages (gold, silver, copper, iron); the fifth answer closes the circle with a loudly proclaimed *"Aequalllllllll!"* sign.

A close examination of the question reveals that while the subject of the riddle, on the literal level, is Dublin, the symbolic overtones point clearly toward H. C. Earwicker. This is hardly surprising, for Earwicker is identified with Dublin almost as often as his wife is equated with the River Liffey, which bisects the city, but there is more evidence than the general identification of man and city to substantiate my belief that on one level the riddle is "about" Earwicker. The connection between burgher and burg is clearly implied by the answer to the third question in I.6: if the pub is to be identified with the city whose motto it bears, it follows that the pub-owner should be identified with the populace of the city. As Dublin functions as a microcosm for the universe, Earwicker is a microcosm of humanity (in one sense he is actually the entire human race); the answers to question 4, reflecting the progress of human history through the ages of gold, silver, copper, and iron, reflect as well the history of the man who is Everyman. Certain other elements indicate that the riddle and its answers describe the "*c*ombarative *e*mbottled *h*istory" of HCE (140.33, emphasis mine). References to marriage and courtship—"the waters of wetted life," "I would be engaging you"—support my contention, developed earlier, that the first four questions in I.6 represent the second (heroic) stage in the circular life of Joyce's universal protagonist, since the characteristic institution of Vico's heroic age is matrimony.

A most significant motif in the riddle and its answer—one which, I believe, represents a primary level of symbolic meaning in the riddle—is the alpha and omega motif, symbolized by several a/o pairings: "*a* dea *o* dea!," "*a*h dust *o*h dust!," "from *A*tlanta to *O*conee," "m*o*y n*a*y n*o*n" (the initial *A* in *"Aequalllllll!"* completes a double a/o pairing). Alpha and omega are probably implied even in "c*a*pit*o*l," since the normal spelling would be "capital." Epstein's assertion that alpha and omega symbolize "*pure* polar opposition"[36] is basically sound, although it should be added that in the circular structure of *Finnegans Wake* the beginning and end are never far apart and are, in fact, interchangeable (note the exchange of the "deltic origin" and "nuinous end" in "Nublid"). In the Prankquean episode, Earwicker plays the part of Jarl van Hoother, who switches from v*a*n Hoother to v*o*n Hoother and back to v*a*n; the alternation represents the Jarl's Phoenixlike death and rebirth as well as the extremes of joy and misery, which Epstein points to,[37] and other polar opposites. The death-and-rebirth theme and polar opposition are closely related: in the dream Earwicker splits into Shem and Shaun who are, as Epstein notes, identified (albeit rather loosely) with alpha and omega.[38] What divides Shem from Shaun is the Park incident—that is, the Fall: *"Shem and Shaun and the shame that sunders em"* (526.14; the context shows plainly that this refers to the shameful encounter in the Park). Significantly, one passage in which the contents of the letter are partially revealed connects the Park affair, the creation of the city, and the alpha/omega motif:

> A pair of sycopanties with amygdaleine eyes, one old obster lumpky pumpkin and three meddlars on their slies. And that was how framm Sin fromm Son, acity arose, finfin funfun, a sitting arrows. Now tell me, tell me, tell me then!
> What was it?
> A . . . . !
> ? . . . . O! (94.16-22)

It seems to me that Shem, in posing a riddle about an "Irish capitol city," is really asking a question about the fall and death of the twins' father. The details of the riddle seem to point this way. Phoenix Park, "the most extensive public park in the world," is the site of Earwicker's fall (it is of course related to the Garden of Eden), but "Phoenix" implies as well the theme of immortality, referring as it does to the phoenix bird.[39] Since Phoenix is also the name of a beer, the Park reference leads to the description of the Guinness brewery: "the most expensive brewing industry in the world." Like all alcoholic concoctions, Guinness Stout symbolizes the fall and resurrection of mankind throughout the *Wake;* moreover, Guinness's is often confused with Genesis, the book of the Fall. The Park incident is related not only to the Fall of Adam but also to the story in which the drunken, naked Noah is overseen by his son Ham (Genesis 9:20-27), and Joyce relates this as well to the Guinness theme: "Sire Noeh Guinnass, exposant of his bargeness" (549.34-35).

The third detail in the riddle, "the most expansive peopling thoroughfare in the world," refers to O'Connell Street in Dublin, a street that Joyce associates in several ways with the Fall. The street is named after Daniel O'Connell, whose career followed the archetypal rise-and-fall pattern that is ubiquitous in *Finnegans Wake*. The blustering speeches (alternating with embarrassing shows of cowardice) of O'Connell's later years, and his sexual lapses, can be found in Earwicker as well. The attacks on O'Connell by the Young Irelanders may be related to Earwicker's fear of the younger generation, while the ownership of a brewery by O'Connell's family (7.12, 382.5-6) is another parallel between Joyce's hero and "The Liberator." Several references to O'Connell and his street strengthen the connection between O'Connell and guilt-ridden Earwicker. Yawn, who is interrogated about his acquaintance with "Toucher 'Thom'" (HCE), is asked if he is "alluding to the picking pockets in Lower O'Connell Street" and replies "I am illuding to the Pekin packet but I am eluding from Laura Connor's treat" (507.26-29). In another chapter a reference to Earwicker's seven-colored suit, which is associated with the fall of Jarl van Hoother (23.1-2), is followed by the parenthetical "(Ochone! Ochonal!)," to which Issy adds a revealing footnote: "And a ripping rude rape in his lucreasious togery" (277.1-2, 277.F2). Two other references to O'Connell connect him to Persse O'Reilly, the name Earwicker assumes when under attack (525.16-18, 580.30-31). The expansiveness of O'Connell Street is itself an important clue: Adaline Glasheen notes that Tim Finnegan, who "lived in the broadest way immarginable" (4.19), must live on O'Connell Street, and she proceeds to note both the theatrical and the Biblical associations of "broadest way"—Broadway, of course, and Matthew 7:13, "broad is the way, that leadeth to destruction."[40] O'Connell Street, it seems, is the road to hell.

While the first three details in the riddle signify Earwicker's downfall, the fourth alludes to the all-important motif of the wake-communion. Earwicker is a composite of spirit and body, both a god—"a dea o dea!"—and mortal man, formed of and returning to dust—"ah dust oh dust!" In his role as Man, Earwicker sins, dies, and is mourned at his wake; as God, however, he is the Eucharistic meal, or drink, served at the wake. The twelve customers in Earwicker's pub—the Morphios in question 7—are the twelve apostles who recreate daily the Last Supper, and Earwicker is both the host and the Host, both Mr. Porter who serves the drinks and the porter which the "god-drinking" ("theobibbous") citizens consume.

Communion implies new life, and Earwicker's "nuinous end" is also the beginning of something "new in us." Beginning and end are thoroughly confused in the riddle: "deltic origin" alludes in part to the delta at the end of a river, and since delta is the fourth letter of the Greek alphabet it may be an appropriate symbol for the conclusion of a four-part cycle. The delta referred to, however, is primarily the triangle, which usually represents Anna Livia or woman in general (note the figure on 293); in question 2, the delta is the symbol for the "mutter." Born of woman, Earwicker comes to a "nuinous end," a phrase which becomes highly meaningful when we realize that Gaelic *nuin* means not only the equivalent of the letter N in the Gaelic alphabet, but also "ash tree."[41] The ash tree, reinforcing the echoes of "ashes to ashes and dust to dust" in "ah dust oh dust!" is also a symbol for Earwicker's sexual "phall." Looked at from another perspective, the ash tree, like Stephen's ash-plant in *Ulysses,* symbolizes the cross on which Christ died.

Once these details are recognized, it becomes evident that, on one level, the riddle describes Earwicker as a type of Christ, moving from his role as God ("dea") to Man ("dust"), from his "deltic origin" (either as a member of the triangular Trinity or as the product of a woman's womb) to his "nuinous end" on the cross. Like every man, Christ recapitulates the Fall of Adam (the cross has traditionally been viewed as a symbolic parallel to the Tree of Knowledge), but Christ lives through the sacrament of communion. The Four who try to solve the riddle are as limited in their perspective as Aesop's blind men: situated at the extremes of the quincunx, they are the gospelers who try to reconcile their views of the life of Earwicker-Christ so as to reach Earwicker at the center of the quincunx, but these four "interprovincial crucifixioners" (377.23-24) never quite manage this difficult feat.[42]

A collideorscape!

If what appears to be a simple question about Dublin yields so many symbolic possibilities as the riddle of the "Irish capitol city," the "collideorscape" riddle (143.3–27), which does not even pretend to simplicity, would provide a team of scholarly explicators with enough material to last for years. Indeed, the passage seems so complex that one wishes for a paraphrase in order to know where to begin, and such a tool is provided in the first two issues of *A Wake Newslitter* as part of an exploration of puns in the riddle.[43] Prepared by the editors of the *Newslitter*, Clive Hart and Fritz Senn, the paraphrase reads as follows:

> now, renewing the cycles amid the odour of modern bacchanalia, if a dehumanised man, worn out by his allegiance to the god of revelry—and tired after a day's work in the city—lies motionless, hypnotised, almost dead, like a giant in the landscape surrounded by the primeval chaos, dreaming of a world of certainty and of his fine heroic son—and at the same time trying to identify himself with Brahman or the Tirthankaras . . . if this man, in a state of suspended animation at the present moment of time—which contains all time—were accorded a close-up picture of all the people and events that have emanated from him and have influenced his life . . . if this man, during the watches of the night, could solve the riddle of being, could see in a single vision the growth and decay of life, the battle of brothers, the acts of birth, copulation and death, what would he seem to himself to be dreaming of and to be? A kaleidoscopic synthesis of all Being.

This paraphrase supports Hart's contention that the ninth question "consists of a discussion of the nature of the dream-situation in *Finnegans Wake* and represents the Dreamer's most honest and directly introverted consideration of his present dreaming state."[44] There is little room here for consideration of the question "who dreams at *Finnegans Wake*?"; a variety of reasonable positions have been advanced,[45] and Michael Begnal has added the interesting possibility that there are several distinct people dreaming simultaneously.[46] For our purposes here, though, Atherton's description of a single dreaming consciousness who represents a "universal mind" is probably the most satisfactory explanation available.[47] Certainly, however, this dreamer identifies himself with the universal hero HCE, and the ninth question is concerned with this man and with his dream—that is, it is a description of *Finnegans Wake.*

The symbol that Joyce assigned to the ninth question is ⊕, which Hart describes as a Buddhist *mandala,* emblematic of "the circular universe with its timeless centre."[48] This symbol indicates the importance of the riddle in relation to the structure and themes of the book as a whole: the creation of infinite variations upon recurring situations and the dynamic stasis of circular structure are among the most important elements developed in the riddle. The riddle pictures the dreamer in a virtually lifeless state ("in the states of suspensive exanimation") in which he sees past, present, and future in the same "auctual futule preteriting unstant," and this condition lends itself easily to a broad consideration of the basic themes of the *Wake.* Among these themes is the paradox of the dualistic universe, a theme central to the relationship between Earwicker (unity) and his sons (diversity): the dreamer is confronted with riddles that examine the nature of the universe and its inhabitants, "what is main and why tis twain, how one once meet melts in tother wants poignings" (143.18-19). On one level the first question asks "what is man and why is he split in two?"—a question that inverts the Sphinx's riddle for man and is clearly related to Shem's "first riddle of the universe . . . when is a man not a man?" (170.4-5). The same themes are developed on another level: since *main* is French for "hand," the question may be rephrased as "what is a hand and why are there two of them?"—a question that returns us to the conflict between dexterous Shaun and sinister Shem or Earwicker's right and left hands (cf. 27.2-4). At the same time the phrase refers, I believe, to the analysis of the letter in I.5: *main* in French means "handwriting" as well as "hand," and the question could well be translated "what is the handwriting like (or whose handwriting is it) and why are there two 'hands' in the letter?" There is, in fact, some evidence that there is more than one "hand" in the letter: the scholar who comments on the text says that at one time it would have been believed that the letter was written by "a purely deliquescent recidivist, possibly ambidextrous" (107.10-11). These interpretations, however, do not even approach a complete explication of the phrase: the second half of the phrase ("why tis twain"), for example, also means "white is twain"—another example of diversity (duality) growing out of unity (symbolized by white light, a composite of all colors).[49] (More frequently, of course, Joyce opposes white to the colors of the rainbow in order to represent the unified and fragmented views of existence.) There may even be a reprimand for scholars who dwell too long on the psychological analysis of literature: *what* (the nature of the work) is the main thing, and *why* (the reasons behind the selection or presentation of the material) is secondary.

The second question, "how one once meet melts in tother wants poignings," reverses the direction of the first question, since it shows Shem and Shaun meeting and merging with each other. (The twins rarely act out clearly defined opposing roles; more often we find that "Heng's got a bit of Horsa's nose and Jeff's got the signs of Ham round his mouth" [143.22-24].) Joyce is of course playing with the idea that tastes vary, that "one man's meat is another man's poison"; the homosexual implications of this phrase are increased by the puns on French *poing* (fist) and *poigne* (grasp) in "poignings." On the historical level the phrase refers to the passage of Poynings' Law in 1494, a law which increased British control over Ireland by forbidding the Irish parliament from considering any measures except those which had already been approved by the English Privy Council and then, somewhat redundantly, requiring the approval of the Council after passage of any measure before it became law. In his account of the body of laws passed by Poynings' Parliament, Edmund Curtis notes that "It was indeed an act of union, a forerunner of the great one of 1800, and intended to link Ireland once again to the destinies and civilization of England."[50] The themes developed here—the melting of one principle, or one force, into another– relate clearly to Joyce's use of language in *Finnegans Wake:* the melting of one word into another is both described and illustrated by the phrase "melts in tother," in which "in the" or "into" merges (or is placed "in tether") with "other" to produce "in tother."

Contradictory structural principles establish the ninth question as the pivotal point in the quiz chapter. The question is both a beginning and an end, the first stage in a four-part cycle (questions 9, 10, 11, and 12) and the last stage in the life of the male hero (represented here by the sleeping-dying dreamer). The riddle begins with the theme of renewal: "Now, to be on anew and basking again in the panaroma of all flores of speech. ..." Symbolically, the question stands for the last (ninth) month in the foetal development of Shem and Shaun, "the wrestless in the womb, all the rivals to allsea" (143.21). The flow of all the rivers to the sea represents the breaking of the amniotic sac, releasing the restless twins (who are already "rivals") from the womb; opposing the birth theme is the allusion to Synge's *Riders to the Sea,* with its theme of death by drowning. In relation to the book as a whole, this question parallels the "Anna Livia Plurabelle" chapter (I.8), in which the flow of the "hitherandthithering waters" is a prelude to the birth of the sons in Book II. The flow of the river to the sea, however, also represents death, as we discover in Anna Livia's final monologue in Book IV. If *Finnegans Wake* as a whole is an extrapolation from the point at which death merges with rebirth, the "collideorscape" riddle encapsulates this moment when "the course of his tory will had been having recourses" (143.12), the Viconian *ricorso* in which cycles of history die and are reborn. Here, as in the simultaneous end-and-beginning of *Finnegans Wake,* death (omega) gives way to renewal (alpha): "shakeagain, *O* disaster! shakealose, *A*h how starring!" (143.21-22, emphasis mine).

Returning to the dramatic situation in chapter 6, we can now appreciate more clearly what Joyce is doing in this crucial passage. Shem, posing the question, asks his brother to suppose that a man, worn out from his daily or godly ("dayety") work, were to fall asleep and see in one instant the universe in its constant state of becoming something else while remaining the same; supposing this, he says, "then *what* would that fargazer seem to seemself to seem seeming of, dimm it all?" This question demonstrates the many levels of appearance through which reality is filtered in the "dimm" dream: while Hamlet knew not "seems," Joyce's dreamer knows little else. Shaun's answer, "A collideorscape," is appropriate not only because of the similarities between the *Wake* and a kaleidoscope, but also because it contains clues to the roles played by the dreamer: he is both God ("deo") and a beast (Old English *dêor*), combining these two poles of his being through his role as Christ the scapegoat ("scape"). At the same time Shaun's answer may be read as a defiant challenge to his brother: deciphered, "collideorscape" offers Shem the alternatives of "collide or escape," the two courses of action between which he vacillates throughout much of the novel. Finally, on a broader level, "collide or escape" describes the melting of opposites into each other and their reemergence as distinct forms.

While in some respects this discussion has barely scratched the surface of meaning in these highly important passages, it has, I believe, focused on some of the more important aspects of Joyce's handling of riddles in *Finnegans Wake*. Constantly the riddles in the *Wake* return to questions of identity and problems of knowledge as the dreamer puzzles through his vision of "all that sort of thing which is dandymount to a clearobscure" (247.33–34). The Finn MacCool riddle reflects the "artful disorder" (126.9) of the *Wake* and, through the generally arbitrary distribution of motifs, suggests both the chaos that precedes creation and the random scattering of the parts of the dismembered hero. Among the hundreds, perhaps thousands, of motifs grouped into this catalogue, the "two and three" motif and other cryptic allusions to Earwicker's sin are prominent, for here as elsewhere the dreamer is simultaneously fascinated and repelled by the nebulous guilt which he associates both with creation and with death. This association is carried over into the "Irish capitol city" riddle, in which the pattern of Earwicker's fall and resurrection underlies the description of his creation, the city of Dublin. Finally the whole dream pattern is synthesized in the "collideorscape" riddle, which, like *Finnegans Wake* itself, is a "clearobscure" riddle for human life and human perception, what man is and what he "seem[s] to seemself to seem seeming of." In various ways, these themes recur in the riddles that I shall discuss in the following chapters.

4

The First Riddle of the Universe

The brother battle that symbolizes all conflicts between extremes in *Finnegans Wake* is nowhere more apparent than in I.7, which consists largely of Shaun's self-righteous diatribe against Shem. Early in the chapter, Shaun cites Shem's riddle "when is a man not a man?" as part of his demonstration of Shem's "lowness":

> [Shem] dictited to of all his little brothron and sweestureens the first riddle of the universe: asking, when is a man not a man?: telling them take their time, yungfries, and wait till the tide stops (for from the first his day was a fortnight) and offering the prize of a bittersweet crab, a little present from the past, for their copper age was yet unminted, to the winner. One said when the heavens are quakers, a second said when Bohemeand lips, a third said when he, no, when hold hard a jiffy, when he is a gnawstick and detarmined to, the next one said when the angel of death kicks the bucket of life, still another said when the wine's at witsends, and still another when lovely wooman stoops to conk him, one of the littliest said me, me, Sem, when pappa papared the harbour, one of the wittiest said, when he yeat ye abblokooken and he zmear hezelf zo zhooken, still one said when you are old I'm grey fall full wi sleep, and still another when wee deader walkner, and another when he is just only after having being semisized, another when yea, he hath no mananas, and one when dose pigs they begin now that they will flies up intil the looft. All were wrong, so Shem himself, the doctator, took the cake, the correct solution being—all give it up?—; when he is a—yours till the rending of the rocks,—Sham. (170.3-24)

While Shaun views Shem's riddle and its solution as evidence that even Shem must admit that the artist is merely a "sham," a close analysis of this passage reveals that much more than Shem's self-indictment is at stake in this chapter: ultimately this episode (and much of the remainder of the *Wake*) dramatizes the struggle of the guilty mind toward renewal. Here as elsewhere Shem and Shaun function simultaneously on two levels: they are actual characters (Earwicker's twin sons) and they symbolize the opposed poles of the divided mind of the dreamer. On the second level, the twins' battles are generated by conflicts within the dreamer's mind. Behind Shem's riddle lies the guilt of mankind—original sin—since Earwicker is Joyce's Everyman; on the level of realistic action, this sin is the obscurely defined Park incident.

Since the episode in Phoenix Park is especially important in relation to Shem's riddle, a summary of the affair and related events will be useful.[1] The exact nature of the incident is unclear, and it is possible that it never occurred at all except in the dreamer's guilty imagination. The first version given is that Earwicker spied on "a pair of dainty maidservants" who were urinating in the Park (34.19-22), but at other times Earwicker himself is accused of urinating, defecating, masturbating, or exposing himself to the girls. Sometime later—perhaps on the following day—Earwicker returned to the Park and was accosted by a pipe-smoking Cad who asked him the time of day (35.18-20). Fearing violence, Earwicker answered, then launched into an elaborate denial of guilt, thereby disclosing precisely what he wanted to cover up. The story spread, and Earwicker became the subject of "The Ballad of Persse O'Reilly," in which the crime was exaggerated to rape: "He ought to blush for himself, the old hayheaded philosopher,/ For to go and shove himself that way on top of her" (47.1-2). With time, the true nature of the event has become irretrievably buried beneath a mass of lies, rumor, and confusion, so that precisely what happened is an insoluble riddle, but the very lack of a definitive version of the incident is what guarantees its status as an archetypal instance of the Fall. Hence Earwicker's "first offense" (34.25) is indistinguishable from the Fall of

Adam and original sin: Phoenix Park is call "Milton's Park" (96.10), Earwicker's tavern becomes *"L'Auberge du Père Adam"* (124.34), and in The Tale of Jarl van Hoother and the Prankquean, which takes place "when Adam was delvin and his madameen spinning watersilts," the Prankquean—an amalgam of the two girls in the Park—is Eve, "the first leal ribberrobber that ever had her ainway" (21.6–8).

One may take two views of the Fall: it may be a *felix culpa,* a creative or potentially redemptive act, or it may be a shameful incident which should be forgotten or denied. In his letter, which appears in as many versions as the original sin itself, Shem, the artist, examines even the most sordid aspects of life and creates art out of filth: though "usylessly unreadable" like *Ulysses,* Shem's letter about the sins of the Father is an affirmation of all life. Shaun, on the other hand, is what Blake called the Spectre or Selfhood, in that he insists on seeing the sexual act as shameful and bestial.[2] His attack on Shem in I.7 may therefore be viewed as an attempt to defend Earwicker by slandering Shem, thereby discrediting his letter about the Park incident. Shaun carries on the attack elsewhere, too, especially in III.1, where he denounces the letter as an unintelligible, slanderous forgery by a well-known disease-carrier (419.20–426.4). In the first two paragraphs of I.7, Shaun introduces several major points in his case against his brother: Shem is unrespectable, vulgar, repulsive, and low-minded, a riddler who devotes himself to teasing, libeling, and confusing decent people.

Like the different versions of Earwicker's sin, Shem's riddle is a major motif-element in *Finnegans Wake.* It appears seven times in different forms:

(1) ... the first riddle of the universe: asking, when is a man not a man? ... when he is a ... Sham. (170.5–24)
(2) ... where was a hovel not a havel (the first rattle of his juniverse) ... while itch ish shome. (231.1–4)
(3) When is a Pun not a Pun? (307.2–3)
(4) ... the farst wriggle from the ubivence, whereom is man, that old offender, nother man, wheile he is asame. (356.12–14)

(5) ...when is a maid nought a maid he would go to anyposs length for her! (495.6-7)
(6) Here is a homelet not a hothel. (586.18)
(7) The first and last rittlerattle of the anniverse; when is a nam nought a nam whenas it is a. Watch! (607.10-12)

In the remainder of this chapter I shall discuss, first, the significance of the original statement of the riddle and its solution in relation to the rest of I.7, and then the other six statements of the motif. Rather than attempting to present a definitive solution of the riddle, I will concentrate on showing the riddle's relation to major themes in the *Wake*.

The First Statement

As "the first riddle of the universe," Shem's riddle is presumably archetypal. The question "when is a man not a man?" involves at least two definitions of "man," one concentrating on externals and the other on the elusive quality of "manliness." The concept of a man who is not a man has several possible sources, but it is almost certain—given the evidence of *Ulysses* that Joyce was familiar with many traditional riddles—that Joyce knew some form of the ancient riddle for a eunuch, which involves some reference to a man who is not a man or only seems to be a man.[3] There are actually two traditional answers to the riddle—"a eunuch" and "a small boy"—so that if one answer is guessed the riddler can claim that the other answer is the correct solution. Joyce adopts this aspect of the riddle tradition and expands it by having Shem's siblings guess thirteen times before he gives them the right answer. In addition, the two traditional answers to the riddle insure a certain amount of ambiguity in the significance of this enigma in *Finnegans Wake,* since it may allude to Earwicker as castrated hero—"Unic bar None" (291.1), "the now waging cappon" (316.34)—or to the sons, who have not yet reached puberty. Analogous to the "man and not a man" riddle is the "nobody and somebody" riddle for a looking-glass: "Look in my face, I am somebody:/ Look in my back, I am nobody.—Mirror."[4] The parallel between these two riddles is especially interesting since Joyce uses mirror-image reversal in converting "man" to "nam" in the final version of Shem's riddle (607.11-12). The looking-glass theme also suggests Issy and her mirror image Maggy and other paired opposites, including dexterous Shaun and sinister Shem.

There are also a number of other possible sources for the riddle. Joyce would have remembered Portia's slighting reference to Monsieur Le Bon, one of her unsuccessful suitors, as "everyman in no man" (*The Merchant of Venice,* I.ii.56); this allusion reinforces the theme of failed sexuality in the riddle. The answer to Shem's riddle, "when he is a . . . Sham," may suggest two more sources. One is the story of Odysseus, who saved his life by adopting the sham name of "Noman" while he was in the Cyclops's cave. The other possible source is the concluding epode in Pindar's eighth Pythian Ode, which reads (in part): "Men are day-bound. What *is* a man? What is he *not?* Man is a shadow's dream."[5] Not only Earwicker but all of the sham figures of *Finnegans Wake,* the dream of a "shadow"—a dying man—are men and not men: they are the unsubstantial projections of the dreamer's consciousness rather than the realistic or "day-bound" figures who live in other novels.

The theme of the man who is not a man spreads in several directions, ultimately implicating everyone. A man is not a man when he is too young or too old for sexual relations, when he is emasculated, or when (like Tiresias) he is transformed into a woman. In *Ulysses,* Bloom's "universal binomial denominations . . . as entity and nonentity" are "Everyman" and "Noman" (*U* 727), and both of these names would serve as answers to the riddle: a man is not a man when he is the Odyssean "Noman" or when, like Earwicker, he is "more mob than man" (261.21). Joyce himself provided another answer in his *Scribbledehobble* notebook: on page 759 of the notebook, in the section headed "Circe," he wrote "God ⊏ 1st riddle."[6] Clearly this refers to Shem's riddle, since ⊏ is Joyce's symbol for Shem, and the placement of this note in the "Circe" section of the notebook suggests that the riddle relates to the theme of "mixed sex cases" (48.2) or sexual transformation. More significantly, however, if the answer to the riddle is "God," the description of the man who is not a man may derive from a heretical view of Christ as divine but not human, a man in appearance but not in substance. In the *Portrait,* Stephen declared that Christ "is more like a son of God than a son of Mary" (*P* 243), and in *Ulysses* Stephen seems to identify with the Gnostic Valentinus, who denied the reality of "Christ's terrene body" (*U* 21). On another level, the "God" implied is the Father, Earwicker himself, whose inadequacies are prime material for Shem's subversive literary production, the letter.

Shem's art is "common to allflesh, human only, mortal" (186.5-6), and the riddle, like the letter, is concerned with man's failures, his limitations, and his humanity. It can therefore be viewed as Shem's attempt to initiate his brothers and sisters into their father's sexual secrets, much like Dolph's attempt to instruct Kev in the secrets of their mother's anatomy under the guise of explaining a geometry problem (293-99). Although Shaun tries to disparage Shem's riddle, it is clear that the riddle represents powerful and dangerous knowledge. Shem's role here, in fact, parallels Satan's role in Eden: tempting his siblings to a fall ("to of all"), he offers forbidden knowlege to the "yungfries" or virgins whose "copper age was yet unminted." The prize he offers to the winner, "a bittersweet crab," is open to a number of interpretations. As "crabapple" (which in fact was the prize in an earlier draft[7]), it alludes to the apple that Satan offered Eve; but since "crab" is also a variety of louse that infests the pubic hairs, as well as cancer (Latin for crab), Shem's prize incorporates not only the knowledge of good and evil but also the diseases that entered the world after the Fall.

In part, Shem's desire to corrupt his siblings derives from the envy that prompted Satan to corrupt Adam and Eve: Shem is jealous of his brothers and sisters because they are healthy and well-adjusted while he, according to Shaun, is deformed

(169.11-20), diseased (422.4-9), and drunken and addicted to drugs (179.20-21). A more important motive, however, is also at work here: Shem (like Satan) attempts to undermine the Father by leading his children astray. On this level, the riddle "when is a man not a man?" refers to the Park incident that proved either that Earwicker is "not a man" (impotent), that he was a "naughty man," or that he was "nought."[8] The interpretation of the riddle as an allusion to the Park incident is underscored by Shem's reference to "the rending of the rocks," a phrase suggestive of castration. During the trial of Festy King in I.4, the phrase appears in a context that alludes quite clearly to the Park incident: "The two childspies waapreesing him auza de Vologue but *the renting of his rock* was from the three wicked Vuncouverers Forests bent down awhits, arthou sure?" (88.25-28, italics mine). The fact that German *Rock* means "skirt" adds another connection between "the rending of the rocks" and Earwicker's crime, which is here interpreted as an act of sexual aggression, possibly even rape.

It is significant that Joyce associates the "rending of the rocks" motif with the fall of Earwicker-Adam, since to most readers the phrase would suggest the death of Christ rather than the fall of the first Adam. Both ideas—the Fall of Man and redemption by the Son of Man—are implicit in Joyce's phrase, which alludes to Matthew 27:51: at Christ's death, "the curtain of the temple was torn in two from top to bottom; and the earth quaked, and the rocks were rent." The allusion is both humorous and blasphemous: the rending of the rocks showed that Christ was "not a man" since it convinced the guards and centurions that he was "the Son of God" (Matthew 27:54).

The "rending of the rocks" or earthquake at the death of Christ closes the cycle of fourteen answers to Shem's riddle just as the thunder of creation or of divine wrath ("when the heavens are quakers") begins it. Since "from the first his day was a fortnight," the fourteen answers represent half a monthly cycle; this cycle must be completed by Shaun, who alone is no more a man than Shem is. At this point neither twin is complete, for it is through their union that they will become one man and replace their father. Hart's comments on the Shem-Shaun polarity reveal something of the nature of the conflict in I.7:

> There are two extremes to the function of this polarity, between which the line of development swings to and fro: when their orbits are in close proximity they war with each other and—at a moment of exact equilibrium—even manage to amalgamate, while at the other extreme there is total incomprehension and a failure to communicate, symbolised by the point of farthest separation of the orbits. The two structural meeting-points are at the coincident beginning and end, I.1 and IV, and at the centre, II.3—that is, diametrically opposed on the sphere of development.[9]

In I.7, Hart observes, the twins are "so distant . . . as to be reduced to the unsatisfactory procedure of hurling abuse from side to side."[10] Virtually all the abuse, though, emanates from Shaun, whose method of attack is blunt, direct, devoid of irony: he attacks Shem mercilessly, retelling and exaggerating his every trespass. Shem, on the other hand, is sly and ironic; furthermore, he sees that guilt (the twins' inheritance from their father) is shared by the two brothers. Admonished by Justius (Shaun) to confess his sins, Shem as Mercius confesses for both of them: "My fault, his fault, a kingship through a fault!" (193.31–32). Shaun, who repeats Shem's riddle as an example of his brother's "lowness," sees only Shem's self-abasement in the riddle and its solution, but a less biased observer must note that here, too, Shem is confessing his brother's "fault" as well as his own: "Sham" is part Shem and part Shaun. Or, as he says at the end of I.6, *"Semus sumus!"*—We are Shem.

The relationship of the twins as half-men may be viewed another way. As I have noted before, Shem, who is frequently represented as a tree, is incomplete without Shaun, the stone, because in their union they become tree-stone or Tristan, overcoming their father, the impotent "Muster Mark" (383.1), through the conquest of Iseult. The castration motif in the riddle is supported by the division of Earwicker into his sons, the tree and the stone, for in sexual terms the separated tree (phallus) and stone (testicles) represent the emasculated male genitals. (This emasculation may also be seen in the sigla ⊏ and ∧, which Joyce used to represent Shem and Shaun: they are imcomplete verions of their father's [E] and mother's [△] sigla.) On this level, then, Shem's riddle is an admission of the impotence of the twins in conflict with each other and a plea for brotherly unity (which Shaun refuses to recognize): neither brother will be a man until the *rendering* of the rocks unto the tree. Separated, the boys are both "semisized" (170.19).

Shaun's misinterpretation of Shem's riddle, which overlooks the reference to Earwicker's "original sin," demonstrates how far the brothers are from union. One source of Shaun's difficulty may be his inability to deal with time. The abundance of references to time in the riddle and its answers relates to the Cad's question about the time of day (35.18–20), which in turn, as Benstock has observed, reminds Earwicker of his nocturnal indiscretion in the Park: "If we are correct in assuming that the sin took place at midnight, noon chimes might well disturb the guilty Earwicker, and a view of Wellington's phallic monument . . . jars him into his confession-denial."[11] Besides the word "when," which introduces the question and all of the answers, references to time and age appear in the following phrases taken from the riddle passage:

> telling them take their time
> yungfries [young fries]
> wait till the tide stops [i.e., wait until the end of time]
> for from the first [from the beginning of time] his day was a fortnight [his day became two weeks (expansion of time); or, his day was night]
> a little present from the past [confusion of past and present]
> their copper age was yet unminted [I.7, the third or "copper" age in the cycle of four chapters, I.5–8, is just beginning]
> when the heavens are quakers [beginning and/or end of a cycle]
> when the angel of death kicks the bucket of life [death as the end of the cycle of life]
> when the wine's at witsends [end of a party or of Mass; if the wine represents fertility this could refer to the impotence of old age; it also refers to Christ's first miracle, at Cana (John 2:1–11), and to Whitsunday or Pentecost, thus to two "beginnings"]

The First Riddle of the Universe 87

when he yeat ye abblokooken [the Fall: when Adam ate the apple; also Yeats as old man (see next reference)]

when you are old I'm grey fall full wi sleep [old age; cf. Yeats's poem "When You are Old"]

when wee deader walkner [Ibsen's *When We Dead Awaken,* hence death and resurrection; the first steps of a "wee" one suggest the beginning of a cycle]

when yea, he hath no mananas [no tomorrows *(mañanas)* means death; the allusion to "Yes We Have No Bananas" (castration motif), and the pun on *mañana,* confuse present and future, for the second line of the song reads "We have no bananas today"]

The importance of these ubiquitous time-references in a riddle about man has been noted by Leo Knuth:

> It is interesting to note that the word 'world' (the Germanic equivalent of Shem's 'universe') is historically a compound noun (OE *weorold,* OHG *weralt,* etc.), composed of two words meaning 'man' and 'time.' Like the riddle of the sphinx, Shem's riddle deals with time (the introductory word being 'when?') and man: 'when is a man not a man?'[12]

The references to time in the riddle and its answers relate to the Shem-Shaun polarity and to the dramatic situation lying behind the dream and the riddle. One of the reasons for Earwicker's undoubted preference for Shaun over Shem is that Shaun is space-oriented while Shem is time-oriented, for the passage of time signifies Earwicker's decline and death. In a later chapter Shem, as the Gracehoper, taunts the Ondt (Shaun) for his inability to "beat time" (419.8), and this equivocal phrase sums up Earwicker's dilemma: having aged, he feels himself losing his sexual powers and, in order to prove his manhood to himself, either commits or imagines that he has committed some sexual act (perhaps exhibitionism) in the Park. When he returns to the scene of the "crime," the Cad's question about the time of day reminds Earwicker of his age. The fact that it is noon ("it was twelve of em sidereal," 35.33) on his birthday ("the anniversary . . . of his first assumption of his mirthday suit," 35.3–4) means that it is the end of two cycles for Earwicker, whose role in society is threatened by the younger man.

On one level the Cad is Shem. This identification can be substantiated quite easily: Shem as Jacob is the "kidscad" who "buttended a bland old Isaac" (3.11); "Caddy," the writer who penned "Blotty words for Dublin" (14.12–15), is obviously Shem as a parody of Joyce himself; and as the Gripes, Shem repeats the Cad's question: "By the watch, what is the time, pace?" (154.16). As Shem, the Cad is both the half of Earwicker's mind that reminds him of his sin and one of the younger generation whom the Father fears. In posing a riddle that refers to impotence and/or sexual indiscretion and is phrased so as to call attention to time, Shem is replaying his role as the Cad, pointing toward the guilt that the dreamer prefers to suppress. The point, of course, is lost on Shaun, whose motive for repeating the riddle and its answer is clear: Shem's riddle is a prime example of Shem's "lowness" presented by Shaun the prosecutor for the consideration of Shaun the judge, who as Justius passes sentence on his brother before allowing him to answer the indictment.

One of the recurring charges in this indictment is that Shem admitted—even boasted about—his perversity. Pulling out a pencil, Shem would tell everyone "the whole lifelong swine story of his entire low cornaille existence" (173.19–20). Creating not out of his soul but out of his excrement, Shem "shall produce nichthemerically from his unheavenly body a no uncertain quantity of obscene matter not protected by copriright in the United Stars of Ourania" (185.29–31); that is, he will write a "dirty book" like *Ulysses*. Thinking perhaps of the "Oxen of the Sun" chapter of *Ulysses*, Shaun charges that the book is a "forgery": "What do you think Vulgariano did but study with stolen fruit how cutely to copy all their various styles of signature so as one day to utter an epical forged cheque on the public for his own private profit" (181.14–17). In the same vein Shaun asks, "Who can say how many pseudostylic shamiana, how few or how many of the most venerated public impostures, how very many piously forged palimpsests slipped in the first place by this morbid process from his pelagiarist pen?"

(181.36-182.3). This passage is rich in "sham" references: "pseudostylic," "shamiana," "impostures," "forged," and "pelagiarist" (the last combining "plagiarist" with the Pelagian heresy).

The riddle and its answer are therefore connected with Shem's writings in two ways: first, because if Shem's riddle is an admission that he is "not a man," as Shaun believes, the riddle reveals the same vulgar self-abasement that Shaun sees in his brother's writings; second, because as forgeries, Shem's writings demonstrate that the author is indeed a sham. Yet as Tindall observes, there is some truth in Shaun's portrait of the artist as forger: "An abstraction from nature, a fiction is unnatural. A departure from nature and its violation, any artifice is false or, as Joyce put it, a fraud, a fake or a forgery."[13] *A Portrait of the Artist as a Young Man,* which concludes with a suggestion of forgery in Stephen's declaration that he will "go to encounter for the millionth time the reality of experience and to forge in the smithy of [his] soul the uncreated conscience of [his] race," begins with an epigraph that, translated in its context, describes the artist as a forger or artificer: "he set his mind to sciences never explored before, and altered the laws of nature."[14] As the representative of "natural man," however, Shaun refuses to accept or understand his brother's preference for the artificial: he speaks scornfully of Shem's preference for canned salmon and pineapple (170.26-32), and his description of Shem's grotesque "bodily getup" (169.11-20) includes references to Shem's "mock lip" and his "artificial tongue."

Potentially more serious is Shaun's assertion that Shem is a heretic, a charge that is consistent with Shem's role as Satan, the arch-heretic. The seventh chapter abounds in intimations of heresy, including "a gnawstick" (Gnostic or agnostic), "national apostate," "antinomian," "Jansens Chrest" (Jansenism), "Albiogenselman," "pantheomime" (pantheism), "pelagiarist," "his gnose's glow," and "armenial" (Arminian). In the riddle passage, aside from the references to Gnostic and agnostic in "a gnawstick," and the obvious allusion to the Quakers in "when the heavens are quakers," Margaret Solomon finds suggestions of three other heresies in the first three answers to the riddle: Jakob Böhme's "alchemical hereticism" in "Bohemeand," henotheism in "he, no," and Arminianism in "detarmined to."[15] The heresy theme is an important element in the riddle and its answer because heresy is a "sham" religion in that it departs from the "truth" of orthodox religious dogma. The problem, of course, is knowing how to tell "who is artthoudux from whose heterotropic" (252.20-21) in a book in which opposites resolve themselves into each other. Furthermore, it seems that Shaun is more intent on slandering his brother than on defining Shem's heresy, so that the effect of the catalogue of heresies associated with Shem is cumulative rather than consistent. For example, it is hard to see how one could be both a Jansenist (who would deny the efficacy of free will) and a Pelagian (who would assert that man's unaided will can bring him closer to God). The contradiction is interesting because it demonstrates that Shaun does not maintain a consistent theological position as Shem's opposite: rather, he shifts from one stance to another, using the language of the theologians solely to defame his brother. One might well demand who is the real sham: Shem, Shaun, or Earwicker. The answer, of course, is that each in his own way is a sham and therefore "not a man."

Besides forgery and heresy, Shem's primary "sham" characteristic is cowardice: Shaun observes that his brother was "cowardly gun and camera shy" (171.33-34). When war broke out, "the scut in a bad fit of pyjamas fled like a leveret for his bare lives" and "kuskykorked himself up tight in his inkbattle house" (176.26-31). Later we are told that Shem

> got the charm of his optical life when he found himself *(hic sunt lennones!)* at pointblank range blinking down the barrel of an irregular revolver of the bulldog with a purpose pattern, handled by an unknown quarreler who, supposedly, had been told off to shade and shoot shy Shem should the shit show his shiny shnout out awhile to look facts in their face before being hosed and creased (uprip and jack him!) by six or a dozen of the gayboys. (179.1-8)

This scene reenacts Earwicker's encounter with the Cad: the Cad's pipe is changed into a gun and Shem becomes the victim rather than the assailant, but the basic situation remains the same. If Earwicker is to be identified with the dreamer at this point, then what is happening is that Earwicker's divided mind is engaged in a defensive shift of roles: his fear of the Cad ("unwishful as he felt of being hurled into eternity right then, plugged by a softnosed bullet from the sap," 35.24-26) is transferred by the Shaun half of his mind to the Shem half, thus at least partially relieving him of his feelings of guilt and embarrassment. The same principle is in operation when Shem is accused of having been a peeping Tom who watched an "impenetrablum wetter" through a telescope (178.26-30; cf. 8.34-36). Again the sins of the Father (the Park incident) are passed on to the son, or to a portion of his mind that he refuses to identify with.

These shared roles help to explain the basic question raised by Shem's riddle: the identity of the "Sham." If their shared cowardice shows that Shem, like his father, is "not a man," Shem's involvement with Earwicker's voyeuristic experience demonstrates that he, too, is a "naughty man." Conversely, the "sham" label that Shaun attaches to Shem applies as well to Earwicker. A crucial ambiguity in one of the opening sentences in I.7, "every honest to goodness man in the land of the space of today knows that his back life will not stand being written about in black and white," has been pointed out:

> While the first reading suggests that "his" refers solely to Shem, further readings indicate that Joyce has a wider reference in mind, namely, "every honest to goodness man" or "every . . . man." This is reinforced by reference in the next paragraph and throughout the chapter to the Garden of Eden. Shem may be a "manroot of all evil" . . . and "the vice out of bridewell". . . . He may be a "sham"—but so is Everyman.[16]

The corollary to this observation is that in his riddle Shem is talking not only about his own unmanly character but about the nature of Everyman, H. C. Earwicker. Throughout the chapter

Shaun betrays his uneasy awareness of the sins of his father through equivocal condemnations of his brother.

While Shaun interprets the riddle and its solution to suit his own preferences, there are ironic refutations of Shaun's one-sided argument even within the riddle sequence. By reversing the order of the last two words in the full answer to the riddle, "when he is a—yours till the rending of the rocks,—Sham," we may derive "sham rocks," a convenient description of the impotence implied by "not a man." Margaret Solomon, addressing herself to this point, comments that "'Shamrocks' contains every ambiguity necessary to understand the passage: organic plant and inanimate stone, parodic fertility, a crumbling church, and, oddly enough, trinitarian oneness."[17] Further, since "the herb trinity shams lowness" (14.34), the image of the shamrock again implies that all three members of the human male trinity—Earwicker, Shem, and Shaun—are shams. Ironically, to "sham lowness" one must first be elevated: the point seems to be that, low as it may appear, the shamrock is emblematic of the Trinity and incorporates the substance of God. The Eucharistic symbolism involved in the "sham rock" is equally ambiguous: while Knuth has noted that "rock" and "sham" are slang for bread and wine,[18] the "shamrock" is also the phony bread of life such as Shem's letter, *Finnegans Wake* itself, or the throwaway that Bloom casts on the waters (*U* 152).

Since the thirteen "wrong" answers to Shem's riddle are more specific than Shem's "when he is a . . . Sham," they illustrate various kinds of shamness that apply to one or more members of the trinity within the shamrock. Certainly the references to time and old age, some of which I have already discussed, allude in part to the downfall of the aging, time-conscious Earwicker. The thirteenth answer, "when dose pigs they begin now that they will flies up intil the looft," probably alludes to Earwicker's fall in the Park: "dose pigs" are the two girls (Spanish *dos* = two, Danish *pige* = girl) who tease Earwicker—"begin" to do something—then fly away. (The girls may also be the source of a venereal infection: a "dose.") A more explicit reference is "when lovely wooman stoops to conk him," which describes the temptress (Eve, the Prankquean, the two girls) who woos man and conquers or bludgeons him. The conquest ends in procreation ("wooman" puns on "womb"), but since "wooman" is ambiguous, the man himself may be the wooer. Perhaps the Prankquean, who "made her wit," "made her witter," and "made her wittest" outside Jarl van Hoother's door—getting wetter and wittier each time—is "one of the wittiest" whose answer to the riddle is "when he yeat ye abblokooken and he zmear hezelf zo zhooken." Again the Fall is implied: giving in to the woman, Adam-Earwicker "ate the apple" of knowledge and discovered that "he's mere(ly) himself"—that is, he is mortal. This knowledge leaves him so shaken ("zo zhooken") that he "smears" (slanders) himself by protesting too much when confronted by the Cad.

The sons, too, are implicated. The second answer, "when Bohemeand lips," seems to refer to Shem, the Bohemian artist, and to his artifice, the *meandro* (Italian: "labyrinth"). But underlying this grammatically incomplete idea is an anagram for "when bo(th) he and me slip," a reference to the inadequacy or failure of both brothers. Shaun, who "points the deathbone" and immobilizes the living (193.29), is probably "the angel of death" who "kicks the bucket of life," but so is Shem in his role as Satan. The "bucket of life" is on one level the womb, so that "the angel of death" could be an unborn child, who would certainly be "not a man"; on another level, the phrase also refers to the death of death, hence to eternal life when man will be immortal and therefore not a man.

Shaun seems to be singled out for attention in "when he is just only after having being semisized," for he is "just only"—just, but not merciful, as when he plays Justius to Shem's Mercius— because he is a semi-sized being, not a whole man. On the other hand, the phrase "when yea, he hath no mananas" incorporates a number of relevant possibilites, including extreme old age or death (no *mañanas*), castration (no banana, no *ananas* [French: "pineapple"]), and spiritual impotence (no *mana*). The pun on *gnomon* in "no man-" suggests geometrical imperfection (note the connection among *paralysis, gnomon,* and *simony* in "The Sisters") and thereby relates this answer to Shem and Shaun, whose sigla are imperfect forms of Earwicker's E and Anna Livia's △ Finally, of course, a man is not a man when he is rude—when he hath no manners.

More important than any of the individual phrases, however, is the basic situation developed in the riddle passage: here as in his letter, Shem offers us a frank appraisal of the limitations of all men, including himself and his brother. Simultaneously he is the tempter and one who comments on the temptation, but since in the cycles of *Finnegans Wake* the Fall is prelude to the Resurrection, Shem's view of the Fall is affirmative, a celebration of the *felix culpa* that contrasts with Shaun's rather priggish attitude. Not only "a . . . Sham," the hero is also, as Knuth has pointed out, *asham,* Hebrew for "sin" and also "sin-offering" in the sense of a sacrificial victim.[19] The pun on "a sham" and *asham* encapsulates the circular pattern of fall and redemption in the *Wake.*

In another sense, the cycle of fourteen answers to the riddle is nearly complete. In the Viconian system that is the primary structural model for *Finnegans Wake,* I.7 is the third (human) age in the second cycle of four chapters (I.5, I.6, I.7, I.8) in Book I. Appropriately enough, the fourteen answers begin with the thunder of creation and end with "the rending of the rocks," an earthquake that begins the human age. Ultimately, the victory here belongs to "human only, mortal" Shem (186.5–6) who, at the end of the chapter, "lifts the lifewand" and ushers in Anna Livia's *ricorso,* the principle of renewal symbolized by the waters of life that wash the dirt out of Earwicker's clothing in I.8. The final paradox of Shem's riddle is the celebration of human effort and failure: a man is "not a man" when he fails and reveals his human weakness, but at the same time this is when he is most "a man."

The Riddle as Motif

When Shem's riddle is rephrased as "the first rattle of his juniverse," the subject is the home:

> And oil paint use a pumme if yell trace me there title to where was a hovel not a havel (the first rattle of his juniverse) with a tingtumtingling and a next, next and next (gin a paddy? got a petty? gussies, gif it ope?), while itch ish shome.
> —*My God, alas, that dear olt tumtum home*
> *Whereof in youthfood port I preyed*
> *Amook the verdigrassy convict vallsall dazes.*
> *And cloitered for amourmeant in thy boosome shede!*
> (230.36-231.8)

The "pumme" is the apple (French *pomme*) of knowledge; here as in I.7, where he offered the "bittersweet crab" or crabapple to whoever solved his riddle, Shem plays the role of the tempter and offers forbidden fruit in exchange for forbidden knowledge. The "fruit" is actually an oil painting ("And oil paint use a pumme"): artistic creation is a form of rebellion against, or competition with, the Father-Creator, and Shem's poem, with its sexual overtones *("cloitered for amourmeant in thy boosome shede")* may be viewed as part of Shem's attempt to expose and replace his father as the lover of his mother. Since all of Shem's writings are of one piece, the poem is a juvenile version of his "farced epistol to the hibruws" (228.33-34), the letter in which he describes the fall of his father. Taken together, the riddle and the poem are a juvenile exposé of Shem's "shome"—a sham home like the one that Joyce described in the *Portrait*.[20]

The "rattle" itself may be paraphrased as "where was a hovel not a haven?" or, more simply, "where was a home not a home?" The predominance of Chuff (Shaun) over Glugg (Shem) in II.1 may account for the shift from "when" to "where" in the riddle, since Shaun is the representative of space while Shem is associated with time. Shem's inability to win Issy, who prefers Shaun, is one element of the sexual and artistic frustration that haunts him throughout II.1. This frustration derives partly from Shem's half-knowledge of his mother's sexual secrets: he has seen her urinate and his Oedipal desires have been aroused—"in that limbopool which was his subnesciousness he could scares of all knotknow whither his morrder had bourst a blabber or if the vogalstones that hit his tynpan was that mearly his skoll missed her" (224.18-20; cf. 262.L2). The poem and the riddle express Shem's dissatisfaction with the home which he once believed to be a protective haven but which turned out to be a sordid "hovel," and they are part of his attempt to fulfill his promise to reveal the secrets of his father's anus and his mother's vagina (229.17-24). The answer, however, is ambiguous: "itch" means not only "it" but also "I" (German *ich*), and "while itch ish shome" can be read as a self-accusation, "while I am Shem the Sham." Perhaps this is appropriate, in view of the prophecy that "Shim shallave shome" (225.14).

There is some evidence that, on one level at least, the riddle and the poem describe Shem's prenatal experience and his unhappiness at being expelled from the womb, the protective haven that was his first home and is now empty (*"tumtum home"* plays on Danish *tum,* "empty," as well as "tummy"). This is the *"boosome shede"* where Shem *"cloitered"* (loitered, or was cloistered, near the clitoris), and the time when "his morrder had bourst a blabber" refers both to his mother's urination and to the breaking of the amniotic sac which resulted in the twins' being expelled into the world. Shem's awareness of the womb as a home is demonstrated when, as Dolph, he vows to make Kev (Shaun) "see figuratleavely the whome [home, womb] of your eternal geomater" (296.31-297.1); the reference to the fig leaf relates Shem's knowledge of his mother's secrets to his awareness of original sin. If the "home" is on one level a metaphor for the womb, on another level it represents Eden (the haven) and the fallen world (the hovel). Read this way, the riddle becomes a question about beginnings and, therefore, ends: the difference between a hovel and a havel is simply the difference between "o" and "a," between omega and alpha. The question, then, concerns the nature of polar opposites in the *Wake* and asks why they differ—that is, what holds them in opposition. The answer, I believe, is that these opposites (such as Shem and Shaun themselves) are polarized through the Fall, through the original shame: *"Shem and Shaun and the shame that sunders em"* (526.14).

Another sundering—the repeal of "an act of union" (585.25)—precedes a later parody of the riddle: "Here is a homelet not a hothel" (586.18). The situation here appears simple: the union of Mr. and Mrs. Porter, which is described in parliamentary terms, is over ("Withdraw your member! Closure. This chamber stands abjourned"), and the failure of sexual relations ("You never wet the tea!") spells defeat for Mr. Porter. The woman, dominant now, establishes her own Home Rule through a set of house rules that are intended to restore order and decency to the household, since "Here is a homelet, not a hothel" (a little home, not a hotel, brothel, hovel, or hot hell). If the earlier riddle discussed the separation of Man from Eden or the twins from the womb, this version indicates clearly that Earwicker's fall in the Park, which is alluded to several times in the list of rules, results in his expulsion from home: the overtone of "home-to-let" in "homelet" warns us of the impending overthrow of the Father as Mrs. Porter cleans house preparatory to renting it out.

Still another form of the riddle appears in the list of the children's theme topics at the end of the "studies" chapter: "When is a Pun not a Pun?" (307.2–3). In the margin next to the list of topics there are the names of such famous people as Cato, Abraham, and Darius. Next to the riddle is Isaac, whose connection with the riddle Knuth explains by noting that Isaac's name, which means "he laughs," is a punning allusion to the fact that both Abraham and Sarah laughed when God said that ninety-year-old Sarah would conceive. Knuth observes that when Isaac was born the name "was no longer a mere pun: God was to establish an everlasting covenant with him, 'and with his seed after him' (Genesis 17:19)."[21] Perhaps that is why Joyce altered this instance of the riddle from its original form, "When is a Paris not a Paris?"[22] In its present form, the riddle has an answer, given a few pages earlier in one of Shem's marginal notes: "WHEN THE ANSWERER IS A LEMAN" (302.R1). Joyce is punning on the catch-phrase "the answer is a lemon," which Partridge defines as a "derisive reply" alluding to "the bitterness of a lemon as an eaten fruit."[23] In *Ulysses* the phrase is associated with sexual infidelity: in the "Circe" chapter Mrs. Breen suggests that Bloom kiss her and, to his shocked reply of "Molly's best friend! Could you?" replies "Hnhn. The answer is a lemon. Have you a little present for me there?" (*U* 446). (The present she is looking at is Bloom's lemon-scented and lemon-shaped soap, which he carries throughout the day.) "The answer is a lemon" may be construed to mean "the answer is something that you would not like to know because this knowledge would prove bitter"; the bitter fruit represents the fruit of the Tree of Knowledge, which is always a sexual symbol in *Finnegans Wake*, and the sexual connotations are increased by the change form "lemon" to "leman."

A clumsy but defensible interpretation of the riddle and its answer, then, might be that a pun is not merely a pun when it conceals a bitter truth about the Fall and when this truth is discovered or answered by Issy, the leman who is the object of the dreamer's incestuous longings. The point seems to be that the dreamer, who attempts to conceal the story of the Fall through the obscure language of *Finnegans Wake*, is afraid that one of his Freudian puns will be heard and correctly interpreted by Issy, the answerer who is a leman. This interpretation is supported by the recurrence of the "answer is a lemon" motif in the next chapter during a retelling of the Park incident: "Wholehunting the pairk on a methylogical mission whenever theres imberillas! And calling Rina Roner Reinette Ronayne. To what mine answer is a lemans. Arderleys, beedles and postbillers heard him. Three points to one. . . . Begetting a wife which begame his niece by pouring her youngthings into skintighs. That was when he had dizzy spells" (373.20–27).

In a different form the riddle appears in the "tavern" episode (II.3), and again the motif is linked to the Fall of Man.

Following Butt and Taff's story of how Buckley shot the Russian General (338.4-355.7), Earwicker speaks in defense of the General (himself) and contends that the sin is not his alone but is universal: "We all, for whole men is lepers, have been nobbut wonterers in that chill childerness which is our true name after the allfaulters (mug's luck to em!)" (355.33-35). Because of the sin of Adam and Eve (the "allfaulters"), everyone must solve for himself "the farst wriggle from the ubivence, whereom is man, that old offender, nother man, wheile he is asame" (356.12-14). Primarily the question here is how Shaun and Shem, who are identified respectively with Plato's Same and Other,[24] are simultaneously identical with and opposite to each other. Having merged together to shoot the Russian General (349.5-7, 354.7-8), the sons now begin to split apart, and the problem of their identities is viewed as a natural consequence of the Fall.

Symbolically, this is a rebirth: the *"abnihilisation of the etym"* (353.22) is the destructive phase, parallel to the Viconian *ricorso,* marking the end of one order and the beginning of another, and once again the twins are re-created and wriggle out of the womb, the "ubivence" or the where (Latin *ubi*) and whence of all life. The riddle, then, can be read as "how can Man be both the Other (Shem) and the Same (Shaun)?" and, more generally, "how can the act of creation result in a dualistic universe?" This is, in a sense, a restatement of the problem posed in part of the "collideorscape" riddle: "what is main and why tis twain, how one once meet melts in tother wants poignings" (143.18-19). Moreover, the fact that both "nother" and "asame" may be read as negatives reinforces the theme of the union of opposites in the true man. This point is further demonstrated by an alternate translation that centers on the roles of the twins as failed suitors, each incomplete without the other: "When is a man not *her* man? When he is only Shaun (the Same) or when he is without Shaun (a-Same)."

Thus far the "when is a man not a man?" motif has been an expression of Shem's view of the Park affair, but the next statement of the riddle, "when is a maid not a maid" (495.6), seems to allude to a different view of the Fall. Throughout *Finnegans Wake* there are two major accounts of the Park incident. The first, Shem's version, is that Earwicker was guilty of voyeurism, exhibitionism, masturbation, or some other sin; the second version is that the two girls deliberately tried to seduce Earwicker and that he has been unjustly defamed. These two points of view are expressed in two variant forms of the letter, the first apparently written by Shem and the second by Anna Livia. The last of the suggested titles for Anna Livia's "untitled mamafesta" states the point of view of the forgiving wife quite explicitly:

> *First and Last Only True Account all about the Honorary Mirsu Earwicker, L.S.D., and the Snake (Nuggets!) by a Woman of the World who only can Tell Naked Truths about a Dear Man and all his Conspirators how they all Tried to Fall him Putting it all around Lucalizod about Privates Earwicker and a Pair of Sloppy Sluts plainly Showing all the Unmentionability falsely Accusing about the Raincoats.* (107.1–7)

Anna Livia's statement of the "when is a maid nought a maid" riddle occurs during the interrogation of Yawn (III.3), in which all the evidence about Earwicker's sin is dredged up time and time again; her voice speaks through Yawn and, at one point, recites a draft of her letter (494.27–495.33). Her plan to "rebuke to the libels of snots from the fleshambles, the canalles," includes an attack on Shem as the author of the other letter and "The Ballad of Persse O'Reilly": "wreuter of annoyimgmost letters and skirriless ballets in Parsee Franch" (495.2–3). Now we learn that Shem's riddle was part of a plot to defame Earwicker: Anna Livia speaks contemptuously of Shem "Sylphing me when is a maid nought a maid he would go to anyposs length for her!"

On its most obvious level the riddle means that a maid is not really a maid, or she does not remain one, when she so excites a man that he would go to any possible length for her—"length" referring in part to the erect penis. The pun on "Oedipus" in "anyposs" opens up another line of interpretation of the riddle: besides the incest motif implied by every reference to the character who provided Freud with his most famous phrase, the allusion to Oedipus suggests the fate of the proud authority figure who searches for the source of corruption only to find it in himself. Oedipus seems to be a laughing-stock to the girls at the *Wake*, for Jaun piously advises all to avoid (or seek?) the fate of swollen-footed Oedipus by putting "your swell foot foremost on foulardy pneumonia shertwaists, irreconcilible with true fiminin risirvition [feminine laughter: Latin *risus* = "laughed"] and ribbons of lace, limenick's disgrace" (434.19-21). The last part of this sentence echoes Shem's description of his father in his first marginal note in II.2: "*With his broad and hairy face, to Ireland a disgrace*" (260.L1).[25] The disgrace stems from the defeat of the father-figure by the Prankquean, whose riddle appears in distorted form in the text opposite Shem's remark. A more complete interpretation of this form of Shem's riddle becomes possible once the importance of the Oedipal theme is noted: a maid ceases to be a maid when she provokes a great sin that corrupts all of society or, more importantly, when she tempts her father (symbolic of all authority figures) to a fall. When a man falls he is "not a man," according to the first statement of the riddle; when he falls because of the shameless temptation of a woman she becomes "nought" (nothing, not, naught) a maid. The close correspondence between Shem's riddle and The Tale of Jarl van Hoother and the Prankquean is illustrated here: a maid is not a maid (or she is a naughty maid) when she becomes a quean or temptress.

At the end of *Finnegans Wake* the old question is asked in still another way: "The first and last rittlerattle of the anniverse; when is a nam nought a nam whenas it is a. Watch!" (607.10-12). If the end of the cycle of life is also the beginning, the first riddle is also the last. Symbolically, then, we are at the end of the life of the hero, and preparing for his rebirth. Time and space are united in "anniverse," and the circular annum-universe, having reached its point of departure, is prepared to begin anew. The importance of time in the riddle has been noted by Knuth, who observes that "a nam" puns on Gaelic *an am,* "the time."[26] The riddle, then, could be translated as "when is time not time? When it is a timepiece (a watch)." The point may be that the circular movement of the hands of the watch, like the circular structure of *Finnegans Wake,* simultaneously records and transcends the passage of time since the circle forms an infinite pattern with no end point. On the other hand, "nam" also means "(I) am not," and functions as the negation of the great "I AM" or God, who is beyond time and timepieces. If this notgod is "nought," it is because he is actually a guilt-ridden ("naughty") man undergoing a symbolic death. The suspension of the riddle sentence parallels the halting, unfinished sentence that Bloom writes in the sand in "Nausicaa": "I. AM. A." (*U* 381). Presumably Bloom wants to write that he is a man, but symbolically he becomes alpha ("A."), the beginning. In the riddle in the *Wake,* alpha is preceded by omega (nought = zero = O = omega) as resurrection is preceded by death.

Dying, Earwicker is no longer a "man" but a "nam"; that is, he is either a man in reverse (possibly because he lives on memories, having nothing to look forward to) or he is a mere name (French *nom*). The clearest indication of Earwicker's impotence at this point is the pronoun "it," which deprives the "nam" of gender.[27] The reversal of "man" also represents the *ricorso* motif of moving backwards; this reverse movement is carried over into the first line of the novel, in which Adam and Eve's Church is described as "Eve and Adam's." Like the last sentence of *Finnegans Wake,* the answer to the "first and last rittlerattle of the anniverse" is not completed, for final judgment must be suspended until the Resurrection, when "nam" will become "man" again and we can ask once more about the inevitable Fall: "when is a man not a man?" Here we are told only to "Watch!"—to maintain a vigil over the corpse.[28]

The motif of the man who is not a man, the pun that is not a pun, the maid who is not a maid, is important not only because of the thematic potential of the riddle but also because it is a multi-level expression of certain technical aspects of *Finnegans Wake*. Working closely with the thematic dimensions of the riddle, the technical elements described by Shem's riddle and its counterparts throughout the book help to justify the oft-heard contention that in *Finnegans Wake* Joyce attained true unity of form and content. The riddle may, for example, be viewed as a description of Joyce's allegorical method: a home is not a home when it is a metaphor for the mother's body, and a man is not a man when he is represented as a mountain or insect. In *Ulysses* the correspondences between Leopold Bloom and a host of historical, fictional, and mythical figures are important, but Bloom is also one man, drawn in realistic detail and clearly individualized. Earwicker is even more the Everyman than Bloom, but he is hardly a flesh-and-blood character in his own right. More generally, however, the riddle alludes to the transformations that accompany the shifting patterns of the dream. The celebrated ending of the Anna Livia Plurabelle chapter, in which the two washerwomen are metamorphosed into a tree and a stone, may be offered as a particularly striking illustration of the transformation of characters into their symbolic counterparts. The transmutation of the materials of the dream is especially important in the case of the motif-elements themselves. Shem's riddle, for instance, is no longer "when is a man not a man?" when it becomes "where was a hovel not a havel," and the question ceases to be a question at all when it is changed into a statment: "Here is a homelet not a hothel."

On another level the riddle refers to the paradoxical language of *Finnegans Wake*. If a pun may not be a pun, perhaps the *Wake*-language is not language at all—"nat language in any sinse of the world," as Joyce puts it (83.12). Joyce is right in more than one way: the language of the *Wake* is not a language in the usual sense of the word, but it is a night-language (Danish *nat* = night) about the "sins of the world"; the many puns on insect names and the frequent confusion of insect and incest may even lead us to describe the language of *Finnegans Wake* as "gnat-language." Paradox is implied even in the title of the book, which means both "the wake of Finnegan" and "the awakening of the Finnegans," and "Finnegan" itself implies the paradox of death and resurrection, since it contains both *fin* and "again." On this level, paradox is the real subject of Shem's riddle, but the answer—"when he is a . . . Sham"—does not mean that paradox is merely an illusion or that it is solely the concern of the artist-forger. Joyce's themes, like the *"O felix culpa!"* theme which resounds throughout the book, are those of real life, concentrated and compressed into a book that is honest enough to look as complex as the reality that it attempts to simulate.

5

Who's Who: The Prankquean's Riddle

Like Shem's riddle, the Prankquean's riddle is a major motif in *Finnegans Wake:* it appears fourteen times in recognizable form, from the initial "Mark the Wans, why do I am alook alike a poss of porterpease?" (21.18-19) to the final "What'll you take to link to light a pike on porpoise, plaise?" (623.14-15). By establishing the basic "shape" of the riddle through its three occurrences in The Tale of Jarl van Hoother and the Prankquean (21-23) and then modifying it in later statements, Joyce develops this riddle into another of the many models for his protean book. The importance of the episode and the riddle has often been noted: Bernard Benstock observes that the tale "provides a clear statement of several of James Joyce's basic themes in the *Wake,*"[1] Grace Eckley contends that "the possibilities of the three-page Prankquean incident are both intriguing and infinite, both contained in the incident and disclosed in the entirety of the *Wake,*"[2] and J. Mitchell Morse has added that the episode is "a small-scale model of *Finnegans Wake*" and that the riddle is "the unrecognizably distorted expression of an inadmissable tendency as deeply suppressed as it is destructive."[3] In the following discussion I will try to take advantage of the episode's function as a miniature of the *Wake* by examining, first, the three primary statements of the riddle in relation to the themes developed in the tale, and then the later echoes of the riddle in the broader context of *Finnegans Wake* as a whole.

The Tale of Jarl van Hoother and the Prankquean

In the Prankquean episode, Joyce's theme of woman as destroyer-creator is demonstrated through a fairy tale version of the Fall: beginning in the Garden of Eden where "Adam was delvin" and ending with the founding of Dublin (whose motto, *Obedientia civium urbis felicitas,* is parodied in the last line of the story), the tale of the "skirtmishes" between van Hoother and the Prankquean encompasses a complete cycle of human history and stands as an emblem for the eternal male-female struggle that characterizes human life. In The Mime of Mick, Nick and the Maggies (219-59), basically the same story is reenacted by Earwicker's children in the form of a game. In both of these episodes the male is given three chances to answer a riddle but fails each time. As a postscript to Shem's riddle, we might add that a man is not a man when he is unable to answer a woman's riddle and pass a suitor test. There is, however, an essential difference between the Mime and the Prankquean episode: while Glugg seeks actively to gain Izod by solving her riddle, van Hoother apparently wants to avoid answering the riddle or dealing in any way with the Prankquean.

Although The Tale of Jarl van Hoother is in many ways extremely complex, the basic "plot" of the story is clear enough. Arriving one night at van Hoother's castle, the Prankquean demands entrance and poses a riddle: "Mark the Wans, why do I am alook alike a poss of porterpease?" On its most obvious level the riddle is actually a request for "a pot of porter, please," but the Jarl, angered at the fact that the Prankquean "made her wit" (urinated) on the "dour" (the door or the dour doorkeeper), slams the door in her face. In retaliation the Prankquean kidnaps one of the Jarl's twin sons, Tristopher, and takes him on a forty-year tour of the world during which time he is converted into his opposite, a "luderman" (a playful Lutheran or a lewder man). Returning with the "jiminy" or twin (from Latin *gemini*), she again appears at the castle, this time demanding "two poss of porterpease." Again the Jarl shuts the door (or shits) in her face, and again she kidnaps a son—this time Hilary,

Tristopher's opposite. Taking Hilary for a "forty years' walk," the Prankquean converts him into his opposite, a "tristian" (morose Christian). Returning with this twin to van Hoother's castle "for the third charm," the Prankquean demands "three poss of porter pease." Whether the Jarl is merely fed up with the increasing requests for porter or whether he fears for the safety of the third member of his household, his "dummy" daughter, he rushes up to the Prankquean, defecates ("he ordurd"), and screams at her to "shut up shop, dappy." Inside the castle the dummy, now called the "duppy" (perhaps to indicate that she is part P-queen herself), slams the shutter shut; the sound of thunder which follows indicates not only the closing of the shutters but also the fall of Jarl van Hoother, who has lost: "they all drank free" with the porter that he refused to give the Prankquean. The result is the signing of a peace treaty, or perhaps the exchange of marriage vows, but in either case the woman is given the upper hand.

The primary source for the plot of the episode is the quasi-historical account of the visit of Grace O'Malley, a sixteenth-century Irish piratess, at the castle of the Earl of Howth while returning to her home in western Ireland after an interview with Queen Elizabeth. The piratess demanded hospitality from the Earl but was refused entrance because the family was at dinner; in revenge she kidnapped the Earl's son and held him captive until she extracted from the Earl a promise that the castle doors would always be open at dinnertime. The Jarl, of course, is a surrogate for Earwicker, as the makeup of his family (twin sons and a daughter) indicates, while the Prankquean is both Anna Livia as a young woman and the two girls in the Park, P and Q, whom Joyce designates collectively as the "Peequeen" (508.26). The kidnapping of the twins derives its force not so much from the Jarl's concern for his sons as from his fear that he is losing his sexual powers and the temptress prefers a younger man; his refusal to open the door to sexual union may indicate his fear of sexual failure although, refusing to recognize the sexual implications of the episode, he prefers to interpret the incident as the attempt of an importunate female customer to enter the pub after hours for one more drink. Yet the Prankquean refuses to allow him to ignore completely the sexual overtones: her references to the Jarl as "Mark the Wans," "Mark the Twy," and "Mark the Tris," recalling King Mark of Tristan and Iseult story, are calculated to remind the Jarl that he, like King Mark, is a rejected suitor and a sexual has-been. If the call for "porterpease" is actually a request for wine (piesporter), van Hoother may have a good reason for refusing the request, for it was a cup of enchanted wine that doomed King Mark's chances of retaining Iseult's love by causing her to fall in love with Tristan.[4]

A cup of enchanted wine played a slightly different (but no less crucial) role in the Irish myth of Dermot and Grania: Grania used the wine to drug the aging Finn MacCool, to whom she was betrothed, in order to elope with Dermot of the Love-Spot (cf. 21.27–28, "the blessings of the lovespots"). This story, which is alluded to several times in the episode, seems to be the single most important source for the thematic implications of the Tale of Jarl van Hoother—the theme of the woman who rejects an older man and chooses a younger and the theme of the woman who divides men against each other. Unlike Iseult, who was trapped in an unfortunate love affair by the cup of wine, Grania not only controlled her own fate but virtually kidnapped Dermot by placing him under solemn bonds or *gaesa* to save her from the marriage with Finn. The incestuous implications of the Prankquean episode—the competition of father and sons for the love of a woman who seems variously to resemble the mother or the daughter—find a parallel in the Dermot-Grania story, for, as Mercier has pointed out, "As early as the tenth century, the elopement of the youthful Diarmaid with Gráinne, the young bride of the ageing Finn, introduces an Oedipus-like theme. . . ."[5]

Various other possible sources for the story, such as the myth of Lilith,[6] have been investigated. One likely source that deserves more attention than it has received is the traditional fairy tale of Rumpelstiltskin. This story incorporates such elements as the three appearances of the riddler (a common fairy tale motif) and the threatened loss of a child as the penalty for the failure to answer the riddle correctly. Rumpelstiltskin's riddle, whose answer is the dwarf's name, is essentially an identity riddle; similarly, one reading of the Prankquean's riddle—one that explains van Hoother's violent refusal to answer the question—is that it is the woman's attempt to remind the man of his sin (of premarital relations with Anna Livia or of incestuous love for his daughter) by forcing him to name the object of his lust, the riddler herself. The Prankquean represents both Anna Livia Plurabelle as a young, desirable woman and her present-day counterpart, Issy; the reference to her as the Jarl's "niece-of-his-in-law" results from the unconscious effort of the dreamer's mind to push the idea of incest into the background by disclaiming any blood relationship with the Prankquean. (This disclaimer parallels Stephen's substitution of "grandmother" for "mother" in his fox riddle in *Ulysses*.) Hence one interpretation of the riddle is that it is part of an attempt to force the Jarl to recognize that he and the Prankquean are closely related: if she is asking "why do I look like I could pass as a Porter, please?", the answer is that she is indeed a Porter (Earwicker's name in III.4), either as the wife or, more importantly, as the daughter of the Jarl.

The parallels between the story of Rumpelstiltskin and The Tale of Jarl van Hoother add another level of meaning to van Hoother's rejection of the Prankquean's advances: the connection between the fear of incest and the fear of conception. In his essay on "The Occurrence in Dreams of Material from Fairy Tales,"[7] Freud reports a dream involving a pantomime in which a strange man (whose actions according to Freud were derived from the dreamer's recollection of the Rumpelstiltskin story) entered the dreamer's bedroom, danced around her, and frightened her. Freud's interpretation was that the strange man represented the woman's husband, that his dance represented sexual advances, and that this frightened her because she feared conception. The Tale of Jarl van Hoother implies such a fear of conception on the part of the Jarl (the male and female roles being reversed): the Prankquean who "makes her wit" before the dour doorkeeper is also making water (like the girls in the Park) and thereby teasing the poor man; when he slams the door in her face he is symbolically closing the path to a male-female sexual union which might lead to the conception of a child.[8] The riddle might in fact be rephrased to indicate a desire to "pass the *porte* [door], please," which in turn would imply a desire for sexual union. The Jarl's masturbation ("laying cold hands on himself," "shaking warm hands with himself") indicates his preference for non-conceptual sexual release.

Although onanism is not the same as masturbation the two terms are often used interchangeably and both acts have the effect of thwarting conception. Thus Frank Budgen's comment about Onan may apply to van Hoother as well: "Onan was condemned not for a contraceptual practice as such, but for a lack of tribal solidarity, of brotherly love. His excessive individualism was punished."[9] It is possible that the Jarl's masturbation and his rejection of the Prankquean result partly from his "excessive individualism" as demonstrated by his refusal to recognize his relationship to the Prankquean or to conform to the communal love practices of a time "when everybilly lived alove with everybiddy else." The continuation of the story of Onan (Genesis 31:12–30), however, returns us to the underlying fear of incestuous procreation; Onan's father Juda lay with Thamar, his daughter-in-law, who was disguised as a harlot (or "quean," to use the Elizabethan term that Joyce adopts). She conceived and brought forth twin sons whose delivery, which involved a reversal of the order in which the sons were expected to be born, parallels the interchangeability of Tristopher and Hilary. Earwicker's continual confusion of the memory of his wife as a young woman with his daughter may explain why he fears an incestuous relationship that (assuming the relevance of the Juda and Thamar story) would produce the twins who are already born; it also helps to explain how both the dummy and the Prankquean can represent aspects of Issy.

The sexual challenge implicit in the Prankquean's riddle is underscored by the knocking at the door. At the beginning of *Finnegans Wake,* Finnegan's feet lie at "the knock out in the park" (3.22), Castle Knock in Phoenix Park, where Earwicker was "knocked out" by the two girl-temptresses. Later, in the "studies" section (II.2), Castle Knock is equated with Earwicker's pub (alias Jarl van Hoother's castle), and the password to the pub is "Persse O'Reilly," the name that is repeatedly associated with Earwicker's guilty adventure in the Park:

This bridge is upper.
Cross.
Thus come to castle.
Knock.
A password, thanks.
Yes, pearse.
Well, all be dumbed!
O, really? (262.3-10)

In II.3, the Prankquean's three attempts to enter the pub (or the castle) are transformed into a knock-knock riddle:

Knock knock. War's where! Which war? The Twwinns. Knock knock. Woos without! Without what? An apple. Knock knock. (330.30-32)

Joyce's explanation of this passage to James Johnson Sweeney is interesting: "He explained to Sweeney that Cain and Abel were the origin of war; the second 'w' in 'Twwinns,' Joyce said laughing, was for Eve, and meant, as the next phrases indicated, 'without an apple,' for she had been born without an Adam's apple."[10] The passage also relates the other apple (of knowledge of good and evil) to the twins, their war, and the knocking motif. In the Prankquean episode the riddle is posed by Eve, the rib-robber ("the first leal ribberrobber that ever had her ainway"), while Jarl van Hoother represents fallen man who makes a pretence of not having the knowledge of good and evil (the answer to the riddle). The Prankquean's insistence that Jarl van Hoother recognize his guilt overlaps Joyce's allegorical treatment of the riddle situation as the temptation of forbidden knowledge, which in turn is translated into the temptation of incest.

The riddle as it appears in the final text is richer and more complicated than the versions that are transcribed in Hayman's edition of the early drafts.[11] The initial version of the first statement of the riddle was a simple request for porter: "I want a cup of porter." This was changed to "Why do I want a cup of porter" and then to "Why do I like a poss of porterpease." The request on the second visit, "I want 2 cupsa porterpeace," was emended to read "Why do I liking 2 poss of porterpeace." On her third visit the "prankwench" originally asked "Why am I like three cupss porterpease,"[12] which eventually became "Why do I like 3 poss porterpease" as Joyce struggled to establish a parallel construction among the three statements of the riddle. Three basic levels of meaning, all of which are incorporated in the final published version of the riddle, can be distinguished in these early drafts: a request for porter, a question about why the Prankquean wants (or likes) porter, and a metaphoric riddle about the Prankquean's similarity to a pot of porter. Certainly the evidence of the early drafts contradicts Frances Boldereff's contention that the riddle originated in Joyce's search for a "point of order";[13] the "point of order" theme is plainly a later addition to the riddle and is less significant than a number of other themes that are incorporated into the riddle.

There are many valid interpretations of the riddle (besides those I have already discussed), each of which demonstrates an important thematic element. Bernard Benstock observes that the riddle "asks the question of the duality of opposites, since the hero's twin sons are asking why do we look like two peas in a pod (but are really as different as day and night)?"[14] Although this interpretation ignores the fact that the riddle is posed by a woman and not by "the hero's twin sons," the "look-alike" theme is of paramount importance in the riddle and applies in part to the twins who appear to be opposites but may exchange roles at any time. Each principle in *Finnegans Wake* bears within it the seeds of its contrary, illustrating Giordano Bruno's principle of *In tristitia hilaris, in hilaritate tristis,*[15] which is the obvious source for the names Hilary and Tristopher.

A more complex interpretation has been offered by E. L. Epstein, who contends that the Prankquean's taunting remark, "Unlikelihud" (made in response to the Jarl's order to stop and come back), may be one answer to the riddle:

> If "I am" [in the riddle] refers to "the great I AM" of Exodus iii.14, that is, God as self-sufficient existence, and the plural form of the verb "do" suggests a multiple God, then "Why do I am alook alike a poss of porterpease?" might be glossed "Why do the three members of the Trinity resemble each other so completely?" In *Ulysses* Stephen has given the Prankquean's answer to the question of the inherent doubt in fatherhood—paradoxically, the Church is founded upon the mystical relationship of the father to the son, a resemblance which can only be known by faith because it is founded upon the void, upon incertitude, upon "unlikelihood."[14]

Epstein's point is that the members of the Trinity are as much alike as peas in a pod not for any logically compelling reason but because Joyce's universe is ruled by "random selection and disorder"—in short, "Unlikelihud." While Mr. Deasy and Frances Boldereff search for a "point of order"—that is, a rational basis for existence—Stephen Dedalus, Joyce, and the Prankquean are drawn to the mystery of existence, the incertitude that, in Father Boyle's words, "does not exclude divine determination but simply makes the purely rational assertion of it impossible."[17] Since within his family Earwicker represents the God of Creation (at least to his children), the riddle also asks "Why does the father look like his sons (the two peas in Porter's pod or home)?" And because Earwicker is the embodiment or synthesis of the opposing forces represented by his sons, the riddle also asks how unity and diversity are essentially the same thing, each growing out of the other—a cardinal principle in the cyclical structure of the *Wake.*

Tindall believes that the nature of the relationship between the Prankquean and the other members of the family is the core of the riddle. He writes that "A.L.P. looks like the twins (who are as like as two peas in a pod) because she is their mother, as 'porter' (H.C.E., the publican, who sells porter and maybe piesporter, a wine) is their father."[18] To substantiate and enlarge upon this point I would offer two translations of the riddle, both of which emphasize the Prankquean's role as the mother of the Jarl's children: "Why am I like a pot of porter, please?" and "Why am I like a pod for Porter's peas?" In either case the answer is that, as their mother, she once held the children (the little "Porters" or "peas") in her womb (the "pot" or "pod"). Concentrating on the Prankquean's alternate role as temptress-destroyer, Margaret Solomon proposes a translation of the riddle which demonstrates the sexual nature of Finnegan's drunken downfall: "Mark I, why am I and a poss of porter as much alike as peas (in a pod)?" Her answer is that "like the porter (ale), she, too, is firewater, and is the cause of man's fall."[19] Since the "firewater" is not only the Prankquean herself but also the urine with which she "made her wit," it might be noted in passing that a riddle about the similarity of the Parankquean's urine and the porter that produces it (the two are united in "porterpease") demands some explanation of the cyclical, repetitive nature of the universe which is symbolized on the large scale by the rain-river-sea-rain cycle and on the smaller scale by the repetition of the process of drinking, assimilating, and eliminating liquids.[20]

One of the more salient overtones in the riddle, an echo of the nursery rhyme "Pease Porridge Hot," has been duly noted by a number of *Wake* critics. Michael Begnal cites the following version of the rhyme, one which is actually a spelling riddle:

> Pease porridge hot.
> Pease porridge cold,
> Pease Porridge in the pot,
> Nine days old.
> Spell me that without a P,
> And a clever scholar you will be.[21]

Begnal's analysis shows how this rhyme relates to the "hot-cold opposition within the tale"; he points out the obvious micturatory implications of "P"; and he relates both the rhyme and the Prankquean episode to the pea-trick or shell game, in which peas are manipulated and exchanged much as van Hoother's sons are. Finally, Bengal connects the "Pease Porridge Hot" rhyme to a similar spelling riddle in the *Wake:* "Lindendelly, coke or skillies spell me gart without a gate? Harlyadrope" (89.18-19). As I noted in my first chapter, this is a children's spelling riddle such as "Londonderry, Cork or Kerry, spell me that without a K." Like this riddle, the "Pease Porridge Hot" riddle is a trick: the answer is t-h-a-t. Pseudoriddle or not, the "Harlyadrope" riddle provides another connection between the Prankquean's riddle and Izod's riddle in the Mime, the answer to which is "heliotrope." The "gart without a gate" is probably van Hoother's garden, but the phrase is ambiguous: does the absence of a gate mean that the garden is completely enclosed, as Begnal[22] and Solomon[23] believe, or does it mean that the gate has been removed? Both interpretations are possible, but the answer Joyce gives favors the former: "Harlyadrope," translated as "hardly a drop," tells us how much porter van Hoother is willing to give the Prankquean, but it also indicates the sterility of a garden without a gate or a man wearing a condom. When Mr. Porter concludes intercourse (or gives up), his wife tells him that he "never wet the tea" (585.31), an indication that the "gate" has not been opened for the transmission of life.

All of this, I believe, relates to the sexual-creative aspect of The Tale of Jarl van Hoother. The Prankquean's request for porter is a metaphor for her desire for communion or sexual union with Jarl van Hoother, but by slamming the door shut, the Jarl rejects these advances. In a sense the Prankquean is herself the porter or firewater, not only because (to quote Solomon again) she "is the cause of man's fall," but because she is associated with the elements of fire ("she lit up and fireland was ablaze") and water ("into the shandy westerness she rain, rain, rain"). Filling out the quota of four elements, Jarl van Hoother represents earth (as the mountain, "mountynotty man," and as the producer of feces which complement the

Prankquean's urine) and air ("van Hoother was to git the wind up"). The combination of these four elements results in the creation of the Word, "the first peace of illiterative porthery [alliterative poetry] in all the flamend [fire] floody [water] flatuous [air] world [earth]." This synthesis of opposing principles begins a new cycle of conflict and reconciliation, for like the *Wake* itself, The Tale of Jarl van Hoother moves in a circle. One obvious translation of "when Adam was delvin" is "when Adam [Earwicker, Jarl van Hoother] was Dublin,"[24] and since the tale ends with the founding of Dublin—indicated by the parody of *Obedientia civium urbis felicitas* in "Thus the hearsomeness of the burger felicitates the whole of the polis"—we end where we began and the episode "moves in vicous cicles yet remews the same" (134.16-17).

Like the *Wake* as a whole, the Prankquean episode counterposes cyclical and progressive-linear patterns of action. Although the second and third visits of the Prankquean are basically recapitulations of the first, there is plainly a change in van Hoother's response to the challenge (and in the outcome of that response) during the third visit. Certain other elements within the story reveal a progression from visit to visit: the most obvious example is the continual increase in the amount of porter demanded. To take another, more subtle, example: on her first visit the Prankquean "pulled a rosy one and made her wit foreninst the dour"; returning for the second attempt, she "nipped a paly one" and "made her witter before the wicked"; on the third visit she "picked a blank" and "made her wittest in front of the arkway of trihump." The change from "wit" to "witter" and "wittest" reflects both the increasing wittiness of the riddler and the progressive wetness of van Hoother and his doorway. But the words also mean "white" (Dutch *wit*), "whiter," and "whitest." The tendency toward increasing whiteness is paralleled by the change from "pulled a rosy one" (picked a red rose) to "nipped a paly one" (picked a pink rose) and, finally, "picked a blank" (picked a white rose). In this episode, the female principle appears to be represented by white, the union of all colors, while the male principle is represented by the spectrum of seven colors. When the Prankquean reaches a state of perfect whiteness (unity) she draws forth the active opposition of van Hoother (diversity): he bursts out of his castle "like a rudd yellan gruebleen orangeman in his violet indigonation," a premature rainbow provoked by the Prankquean's flood.

It is often asserted—but rarely demonstrated—that The Tale of Jarl van Hoother and the Prankquean is structured according to the Viconian system.[25] Although the extreme complexity of the episode renders absurd the attempt to assign any part of the story exclusively to one Viconian age, the general pattern of development in the story is certainly Viconian. In each age the posing of the riddle is the event that, by challenging the status quo, stimulates the Jarl into action and produces a cosmic disturbance which in turn introduces a new age. Specifically, the divine age (which runs roughly from 21.5 to 21.26) is indicated by the presence of Adam and Eve (21.6–8), the first people in *Finnegans Wake* (3.1) as well as in the Bible; by the free-love practices of an innocent, prelapsarian society (21.9); by the introduction of fire—allegorically the introduction of the knowledge of good and evil—by the promethean Prankquean (21.16–17); and by the fall of the angels (21.25). (At the end of the next era—22.12—there are "starshootings" rather than "falling angles," which seems to indicate a change from the primitive, poetic attitude toward the cosmos to a more rationalistic viewpoint.) The heroic age is indicated by the reference to van Hoother's "baretholobruised heels" (21.35) which shows, I think, that he shares Achilles' weakness; there is also an allusion to Brodhar or Brodir, the Norseman who slew Brian Boru after the Battle of Clontarf (22.2). The introduction of the knowledge of good and evil through the posing of the riddle during the first visit has had its effect, too: formerly called the "dour," van Hoother is now the "wicked." The reference to Grania and the second cosmic upheaval (22.12) bring the heroic age to an end. The conversion of Hilary into a Cromwellian Puritan (22.14–17) introduces the human or democratic age, which ends with the thunder of fall and creation and is followed by a brief period of peace.

The tripartite structure in this episode resembles the pattern of a common mythic motif: the task which the hero fails to complete on the first two tries before succeeding on the third attempt. Combinations of threes appear throughout oral literature: Beowulf, for example, slays three monsters and is himself killed by the third, while the number three has particular importance in the *Iliad*. In medieval Irish literature the number three appears quite frequently and assumes a kind of ritualistic significance. The story of "Bricriu's Feast" consists essentially of a series of tests put to three men to decide who has the right to the choicest portion of the feast that Bricriu lays out. In the version of Dermot and Grania story recorded by Cross and Slover,[26] Dermot challenges a group of men who are seeking him to perform three feats (one a day for three days); he defeats and binds three enemy chiefs; he and his companions fight off attacks from three hounds and then three men; and in a particularly amusing scene Dermot, who is hiding in a berry tree under which Finn and Ossian are playing chess, saves Ossian from imminent defeat and gives him the game three consecutive times by dropping a berry on the piece that Ossian must move in order to win the game. In the end it is the failure of Dermot's three attempts to kill a boar (with his dog, his javelin, and his sword) that results in the wound that kills him, and although Finn makes three trips to the well whose waters hold the only cure for Dermot, the first two attempts fail because the water runs through Finn's hands and Dermot dies before Finn arrives with the water on the third trip.

Like Dermot, Cuchulain was doomed by a combination of threes: following an encounter with three crones, who force him to break a taboo, Cuchulain is assailed by a satirist who challenges him three times to give up his spear. There is even a riddle of sorts involved: each time Cuchulain gives up his spear it is thrown back and the satirist predicts that a "king" will die by that spear. The first king to die is Loeg ("king" of charioteers); the second time it is Cuchulain's horse, the Gray of Macha ("king" of horses); finally, it is Cuchulain, king of warriors, who dies. Like the man who challenged Cuchulain, the Prankquean is really a druidic satirist, for the satirists were fond of pulling pranks and were able to perform magical conversions; posing the riddle three times, she is not only challenging van Hoother's wit but also threatening him with exposure through a satiric poem such as "The Ballad of Persse O'Reilly."

If the *Wake* is Joyce's model of the universe, The Tale of Jarl van Hoother and the Prankquean is a model of *Finnegans Wake*, a demonstration piece in which Joyce records a number of his most important themes. By structuring the episode, like the book, on the three ages of a Viconian cycle of history, from the Garden of Eden to the founding of Dublin, and at the same time reproducing the tripartite structure of a mythic action involving one cast of characters, Joyce turns the episode into a ritualistic action of cosmic significance. Not only the Mime but a number of other episodes in the *Wake* follow the pattern set by The Tale of Jarl van Hoother, thereby establishing this tale as an archetypal action. Like the repetition of a religious formula—e.g., the "Sanctus! Sanctus! Sanctus!" phrase which Joyce parodies at least thirteen times in the *Wake*—the division of an action into three basically similar stages, each accompanied by a key phrase (the riddle), is a means of ritualizing that action. "I have your tristich now; it recurs in three times the same differently," Joyce explains (481.10-11), and this paradoxical description applies not only to human life but to God as well. In fact, the Viconian ages may be applied quite easily to the three persons of the Trinity. God appears first as the Father, issuing arbitrary commands and frightening primitive man into blind obedience. Next, God appears as the Son, a hero who triumphs over Satan (cf. *Paradise Regained)* and even undergoes the epic descent into the underworld. Finally, God appears as the Holy Ghost, the paraclete who intercedes for man. In this last stage, God is neither divine dictator nor hero, but the source of grace which is dispensed through human authority.[27]

These correspondences, I believe, relate the Prankquean's riddle to the technical and philosophical bases of the *Wake*. I have already cited Epstein's gloss on the riddle, "Why do the members of the Trinity resemble each other so completely?" The Prankquean might also be asking why all actions and all beings—whether man or god, in any of the Viconian ages—resolve themselves into the same archetypal patterns (such as those in the tale itself). Campbell and Robinson observe that "The point [of the Prankquean episode] is, that this folk tale, selected at random, discloses, as does everything else in the world, the traits of our guilty hero and his fall. All conforms to the family pattern of HCE, ALP, their daughter, and their twins."[28] This seems to be what Joyce is saying when he comments that "it recurs in three times the same differently," from "the human historic brute, Finnsen Faynean" to "Mr Tupling Toun of Morning de Heights" (481.10–15). In the next paragraph, Joyce refers explicitly to the Trinity and the great I AM: "Petries [*patris*] and violet ice [*filius*] (I am yam . . . meaning Dodgfather, Dodgson and Coo [God-Father, God-Son, and dove as symbol of the Holy Ghost]) and spiriduous sanction [*spiritus sancti*]!" (481.35–482.2). Even the Trinity itself conforms to the pattern of HCE, Shaun, and Shem, while Issy and ALP at various times play the roles of Eve and Mary. Jarl van Hoother, of course, plays the role of the Father, a role reinforced by his initials (JVH), which reflect the Tetragrammaton (JHVH); Father Boyle adds that the initials also suggest Jahveh (Father), *V*erbum (Son), and *H*oly Ghost.[29]

In view of these theological overtones, I believe that two more interpretations of the riddle may be offered: "Why does the Trinity [God=I AM] resemble the people in Porter's place?" and "Why is the Trinity like a pot of porter, please?" The first question involves Joyce's anthropomorphic conception of the Trinity, which in turn relates to the Hermetic correspondences that form the basis for the allegory in *Finnegans Wake*. The second question is actually more complex: the point seems to be that, just as eternity may be present in any instant in the *Wake*,[30] all of God is present in any of his creations, especially in the porter that Earwicker serves—the equivalent of the Eucharistic wine. In the last chapter I noted the Eucharistic symbolism in the "rocks" (bread) and "Sham" (wine) of the answer to Shem's riddle. Here Joyce develops at least two levels of symbolic parallels for the bread and wine. On the broad level, the porter represents the wine, while Earwicker-van Hoother (in his role as the egg which is eaten at the wake) is himself the bread. Scatological parallels may be found in the Prankquean's urine (a waste product derived from the porter) and van Hoother's ordure (23.4: "he ordurd"). Both are representations of God, the Word (John 1:1), since the urine is also the Prankquean's "wit" and "ordure" puns on Danish *ord,* "word."[31] Finally, if the feces and urine are the bread and wine, both Jarl van Hoother and the Prankquean are "like a pot of porter," for they contain the Eucharistic material that is the source of life, the symbol for the mystery of life, and the transmuted substance of the Trinity.

Echoes of the Prankquean's Riddle

Oddly enough, the first of the later instances of the riddle has seldom been identified as an occurrence of this motif. It appears during a mock-psychoanalytic investigation of the letter in which the Park episode is viewed from another angle:

> Some softnosed peruser might mayhem take it up erogenously as the usual case of spoons, *prostituta in herba* plus dinky pinks deliberatively summersaulting off her bisexycle, at the main entrance of curate's perpetual soutane suit with her one to see and awoh! who picks her up as gingerly as any balmbearer would to feel whereupon the virgin was most hurt and nicely asking: whyrc have you been so grace a mauling and where were you chaste me child? Be who, farther potential? (115.13–21)

The girl's arrival at the gate, the man's emergence in response to her action, and the reference to Grace O'Malley relate this passage to the Prankquean story. The use of "curate" in Dublin slang to mean bartender ("Let... the curate [be] one who brings strong waters"—116.16-19) implies another connection between the man in this incident and van Hoother, while the primary meaning of the term suggests that the "farther potential" is a priest hearing the girl's confession.

His question "whyre have you been so grace a mauling and where were you chaste me child?" is ambiguous: "grace a mauling" may mean that she was in a state of grace, or that she was Grace O'Malley, who mauled the Earl of Howth, or that she herself was mauled and was grateful for it, while *chaste* puns on *chased* and thereby implies a dual vision of woman as virgin and temptress. Perhaps more important than the specific meaning of the riddle, however, is the reversal of one of the key elements in the Prankquean story, since here it is the man rather than the woman who holds the power and secret knowledge represented by the riddle. As one of the many re-creations of the Park affair, this passage illustrates the perfect ambiguity of the incident: Earwicker may be viewed as victim or aggressor, the girl as prostitute or virgin, depending on how we read the letter. Like the riddle, the archetypal event has no definitive version, only a basic structure than can be modified in any of a number of ways and that carries with it various overtones and associations.

The riddle reappears in the Mime episode in the paragraph that describes Glugg's (Shem's) earliest memory of his mother (224.9-21). Glugg has seen his mother tempting his father (Jarl van Hoother) and has seen the man lighting up, in anger or in sexual excitement, while "she sprankled his allover with her noces of interregnation: How do you do that lack a lock and pass the poker, please?" The urination motif implied by "sprankled" recalls the Prankquean's temptation of Jarl van Hoother and, of course, Earwicker's encounter with the two girls in the Park. Several meanings of "noces" support and extend this interpretation: as "mystical knowledge" (gnosis) it is both the forbidden knowledge whose pursuit gets Earwicker into trouble and the knowledge of this incident which inspires

Shem to write his letter (cf. 182.4-29); as "nuptials" (French *noces*) it describes the wedding that results when man gives in to temptation; and as "night" (Latin *nox,* Spanish *noches*) it refers to the time that the incident apparently took place (the Prankquean's second visit came "lace at night"—21.33). In the riddle Anna Livia seems to remind her husband of the fall of the Jarl by observing that he lacks a lock (hence his inability to refuse the Prankquean entrance to his castle); the request to "pass the poker, please" is obviously sexual, especially since elsewhere Anna refers to Earwicker's penis as "his propendiculous loadpoker" (493.10). Far from being the wife's attempt to establish sexual relations with her husband, however, the riddle refers to his decline and fall: "lack a lock" puns on "lack a lot" (with perhaps an ironic reference to Launcelot), while "interregnation" includes both "inter" (the burial of the fallen hero) and "interregnum" (the period between Earwicker's burial and resurrection). Whatever the true significance of the event, it appears that Glugg's memory of his mother's actions—buried in his "subnesciousness" (224.17)—is responsible for his failure to answer Izod's heliotrope riddle: "It was so said of him about of his old fontmouther. Truly deplurabel!" (224.9-10).

At the beginning of the next chapter (II.2), Joyce extends the range of meanings in an already overly rich motif. The question is one of locations, but ultimately it is related to the problem of creation:

> As we there are where are we are we there from tomtittot to teetootomtotalitarian. Tea tea too oo.
> Whom will comes over. Who to caps ever. And howelse do we hook our hike to find that pint of porter place? Am shot, says the bigguard. (260.1-7)

The riddle here works on several levels. On the naturalistic level the children are assembled in their room over the tavern, and the "pint of porter place" that they hear is actually a customer's call for a "pint of porter, please." Within the context of the children's studies, however, the riddle states the problem of defining one's position in relation to the rest of the universe: the children ask "how do we find the pub (Porter's place, the place where pints of porter are served)?" The reference to Tom Tit Tot, who in Suffolk folklore plays the part of Rumpelstiltskin, reminds us of the Prankquean's identity riddle and suggests that in the riddle the Porter children are trying to "find themselves."

The marginal comments by the children open up further possibilities. Shaun proclaims that the question under consideration is "UNDE ET UBI" or "whence and where"; Shem, less pious, describes his father: *"With his broad and hairy face, to Ireland a disgrace";* Issy adds that "If old Herod with the Cormwell's eczema was to go for me . . . I'd do nine months for his beaver beard." I have already observed that Shem's marginal note ties Earwicker to the "swell foot," Oedipus (cf. 434.19–21), and certainly the incest motif is stated plainly enough in Issy's comment. The phrase "hook our hike" in the riddle introduces another sexual motif: "hook and eye," which is often substituted for "how can I" (e.g., at 62.24); in the washerwomen's conversation about HCE and ALP, this motif appears as "And if they don't remarry that hook and eye may! O, passmore that and oxus another!" (197.16–17). The hook and eye represent closeness (Partridge defines the phrase as "Arm in arm"[32]), and the symbolism of the hook and eye seems in particular to refer to sexual relations. Sexual creation is the UNDE—the answer to the question of origins—that Shaun was seeking, but if the riddle asks, on one level, the question of the origin of life and the nature of procreation, the overtone of "how can I" reflects the sexual immaturity of the twins.

Typically enough, Shaun interprets the riddle as a philosophical problem while Shem treats it as a joke at his father's expense. Issy, however, knows more than her brothers: she is the budding temptress who will play the Prankquean's role in the next generation, and her own version of the riddle emphasizes the incest motif—the idea of the suitor-kin: "And she had to seek a pond's apeace to salve her suiterkins. Sued!" (301.F1). Issy's riddle reminds one of the outcome of the Prankquean episode—the salvation of van Hoother through the peace treaty and his submission to the Prankquean—but, more importantly, it describes Issy's efforts to reconcile her warring brothers, her "suiterkins." The question of identity that is so important in the original version of the riddle is restated here: the echo of "a pod of peas" in "a pond's apeace" returns us to the constant problem of the duality of the brothers who are opposites yet are alike as two peas in a pod.

Issy's version of the riddle predominates through the story of the Norwegian Captain in II.3, as "suiterkins" is modified to "sowterkins" (311.23), "solder skins" (317.22), and, finally, "saussyskins" (324.12) in three versions of the riddle. Since the episode as a whole (311-32) is one of the most complex sections of *Finnegans Wake,* it may be useful to review some background information before treating these riddles. There are many apparent similarities between this story and The Tale of Jarl van Hoother: besides the three parodies of the Prankquean's riddle, these include references to "a queen of Prancess" (312.22) and to the "P and Q" motif (314.19-20); the Captain's three appearances at the pub and his two disappearances—once for "Farety days and fearty nights" (312.9-10), paralleling the Prankquean's forty-year walks with Tristopher and Hilary; the three christenings of the Captain (320.6-10), which recapitulate the Prankquean's conversions of the twins; several minor motifs, such as "they all drank tea (or made free)," which appear in both stories (23.7-8, 330.25-26, 332.2-3); and the marriages at the conclusions of the two episodes.

The basic plot of the Norwegian Captain story is familiar to readers of Ellmann's biography, since the source of the tale is the story, told by Philip McCann and embellished by John Joyce, about "a hunchbacked Norwegian captain who ordered a suit from a Dublin tailor, J.H. Kerse.... The finished suit did not fit him, and the captain berated the tailor for being unable to sew, whereupon the irate tailor denounced him for being unable to fit."[33] In *Finnegans Wake* the Captain arrives, orders a suit of clothes, and departs without paying; to the enraged demand of the Ship's Husband that he "Stolp, tief, stolp, come bag to Moy Eireann!" he echoes the Prankquean's reply to a similar command: "All lykkehud!" (312.1–3). The Captain returns (315.21) and orders a feast at the tavern run by the Ship's Husband (317.11); now interested in the daughter of the Ship's Husband, he is beginning to lose his wanderlust (318.9–10). The daughter is young Anna Livia Plurabelle, as the references to her initials and to her symbol (△) indicate (318.12–13), but the Captain is not yet ready for married life so he sails, once again, without paying the bill (320.23–25). For a while Kersse the Tailor, the Captain's rival in love, holds the stage, but the Captain returns (324.11), is baptized an Irish Catholic (326.6–8), and eventually married—"Cawcaught. Coocaged" (329.13). (The caw and the coo belong to the raven and the dove, who are not only Issy and her mirror image but also P and Q, the two girls in the Park, who unite in the figure of the Prankquean.)

Obviously this is only a basic reading of the "plot" of the episode; furthermore, the narrative level is far from clear, for it is not always possible to distinguish between what happens in the story and what happens in the pub where the tale is being told. Problems of interpretation are compounded by the way the people in the story play more than one role. It is obvious that, on one level, Earwicker and the Captain are one: it is the Captain's hump of guilt, which Earwicker shares, that makes him hard to fit. On the other hand, Kersse is identified with two of Earwicker's surrogates; not only does he wear Finn MacCool's "white hat" (322.1, 322.5), but he is also identified with Persse (O'Reilly) through the P/K Split, the tendency for initial "p" sounds in Indo-European words to be converted into initial "k" sounds in the Goidelic or C-Celtic branch of the Celtic language group, which includes Irish Gaelic.[34] The roles of both sailor and tailor as Earwicker, however, resolve easily into an identification of the two with the twins: the Captain replays Shem's (Glugg's) role in the Mime by running away and sending a telegram (315.32–33), and later he goes into exile "down under" in Australia, which Shem often visits (321.32). Conversely, Shaun's curse on his brother is implied in Kersse's name—"And kersse him, sagd he" (320.2)—and Shaun is the primary representative of the bourgeois mercantile class to which Kersse belongs. Three basic interpretations of the symbolic action may be offered. On one level the Captain is Earwicker as a young man, succumbing to the charms of Anna Livia and defeating a rival—Kersse—for her love. This event is confused in the dreamer's mind with another, more recent adventure: the Park incident. On this level the Ship's Husband's daughter splits into two (the raven and the dove) and tempts the Captain (Earwicker), while the three tailors (315.11, 317.22-26) play the roles of the soldiers who witness the event. Finally, on another level, the Ship's Husband (who keeps a pub) is Earwicker as father, while the Captain and Kersse are the brothers who fight over their sister (Issy, daughter of the Ship's Husband).

The echoes of the Prankquean's riddle, forming the frame for the story, indicate that the action of the story parallels that of the Prankquean episode, but certain elements imply a reversal of the male and female roles. Although it is the Captain who comes and goes like the Prankquean, in the end it is he who is "Cawcaught" and "Coocaged" like Jarl van Hoother. Furthermore, only the first of the three statements of the riddle is the Captain's; the second is stated by the first of the three tailors and the third by the narrator. The initial version of the riddle plunges the reader into the basic plot of the story:

> —Then sagd he to the ship's husband. And in his translatentic norjankeltian. Hwere can a ketch or hook alive a suit and sowterkins? Soot! sayd the sayd the ship's husband, knowing the language, here is tayleren. (311.21-24)

Obviously enough, the basic question is "where can I get a suit of clothes?" As a request for directions to a tailor, the Captain's question parallels the earlier statement of the riddle (260.5-6) in which the twins seek directions to "that pint of porter place"; another parallel between these two versions of the riddle is the "hook and eye" motif ("hook our hike," "hook alive"), which symbolizes sexual union. The union here may be a homosexual one, as Margaret Solomon believes,[35] but it is also a preparation for heterosexual courtship: the Captain wants a love-suit ("clothse for his lady," 311.28) which will help him "hook" a woman. The ever-present incest motif is implied in the echo of Issy's "suiterkins" in "sowterkins," an indication that the suit is directed at the suitor's kin; the Ship's Husband, at least, sees something dirty about the Captain's "Soot!" Here again, as in the Mime, the courtship of Issy is delayed because the brothers are impotent except when united; further, the Captain seems to be castrated since he is described as a capon (316.34).

The second echo of the riddle appears when the three tailors grumble over the bad behavior of the Captain, who has reappeared and has ordered a huge meal without paying for the suit:

—Nohow did he kersse or hoot alike the suit and solder skins, minded first breachesmaker with considerable way on and
—Humpsea dumpsea, the munchantman, secondsnipped cutter the curter.
—A ninth for a ninth. Take my worth from it. And no mistaenk, they thricetold the taler and they knew the whyed for too. (317.22-27)

The tailors seem intent on creating a "breach" between the Captain (who is now called the "taler" to indicate that the tale-telling Captain and Kersse the Tailor are really one) and Kersse: "And three's here's for repeat of the unium [repeal of the union]!" (317.29). While the first tailor observes that the Captain had not cursed or hooted about the ill-fitting suit he ordered on his first visit, the tailors are also the three soldiers in the Park commenting on Earwicker's fall (cf. 314.10-14). Similarly, the antagonism between the Captain and Kersse represents the split in Earwicker's mind caused by the fall in the Park. The first tailor-soldier notes Earwicker's impotence—the failure of his "suit" which now has a breach in the breeches; the second compares the sea rover to Humpty Dumpty; and the third asks for retribution for the crime (an eye for an eye).

The third echo of the Prankquean's riddle in the Norwegian

Captain episode comes when, following a discussion of the Park incident by the customers, the Captain reenters the pub:

> ... his tail toiled of spume and spawn, and the bulk of him, and hulk of him as whenever it was he reddled a ruad to riddle a rede from the sphinxish pairc while Ede was a guardin, ere love a side issue. They hailed him cheeringly, their encient, the murrainer, and wallruse, the merman, ye seal that lubs you lassers, Thallasee or Tullafilmagh, when come of uniform age.
> —Heave, coves, emptybloddy!
> And ere he could catch or hook or line to suit their saussyskins, the lumpenpack. Underbund was overraskelled. As
> —Sot! sod the tailors opsits from their gabbalots, change all that whole set. Shut down and shet up. Our set, our set's allohn. (324.4–16)

The Captain is beginning to age, as the reference to the Ancient Mariner indicates, and he bears his share of guilt: he is Oedipus, who solved the Sphinx's riddle; Adam, from whom Eve came as "a side issue"; and HCE, returned from emptying his bladder ("*H*eave, *c*oves, *e*mptybloddy!") in Phoenix Park ("sphinxish pairc"). Although he is hailed when he enters, the Captain is immediately told to sit down and shut up so the customers can listen to the radio; apparently this Viking invasion poses no threat to the customers. The "riddle" has actually lost its force as a challenge and is now a statement about the Captain's inability to move quickly, but the repetition of the motif satisfies Joyce's concern for a structural parallel between the present episode and other tripartite episodes that are patterned after the story of the Prankquean. The third appearance of the familiar rhythm in this story warns the reader that the Fall is near.

A more important statement of the riddle is heard at closing time. A new version of Hosty's "Ballad of Persse O'Reilly" is being composed by the irate customers, who resent being put out, and the ballad predicts the triumph of youth over old age and the downfall of Earwicker (371.6–373.11). In the midst of this confusion Earwicker is reminded of the Park incident—here represented as a reenactment of the fall of Jarl van Hoother:

> Now is it town again, londmear of Dublin! And off coursse the toller, ples the dotter of his eyes with her: Moke the Wanst, whye doe we aime alike a pose of poeter peaced? While the dumb he shoots the shopper rope. And they all pour forth. (372.2-6)

The theme of the Fall is invoked here through several allusions: the last two sentences echo the phrases surrounding the thunder-word which signals van Hoother's downfall ("And the duppy shut the shutter clup. . . . And they all drank free," 23.5-8), and the "toller" is not only Kersse but a bell (or bell-ringer) that tolls out Earwicker's doom. The phrase "the dotter of his eyes" identifies the riddle-poser as Issy (the daughter), and the substitution of "daughter" for "apple" in the catch-phrase "the apple of his eye" equates Issy with the apple or forbidden fruit. The sexual implications of this substitution are increased by the allusion to the "dot the 'i'" motif, which, as Hart observes, carries "phallic, as well as pedagogic" connotations.[36] Another phrase, "poeter peaced," alludes to the creation of the Word—"the first peace of illiterative porthery" in the world (23.9-10)—and implies the identification of the Word with the sacramental porter that Earwicker serves and embodies, as well as with the poet and his creation. Issy, however, seems to accuse Earwicker of only posing as the poet-creator ("pose of poeter peaced"); perhaps, like Shem, Earwicker is a forger, or—if the creation implied is sexual as well as artistic—he is a cuckold, but in any case the "pose" and the overtone of "mock" in "Moke" stamp Earwicker as a sham. At the same time, "pose" may be used in the sense of "poser"—a puzzling question—so that Issy's question may be paraphrased "Why are we (women) like a poser or an enigma?" or "Why do we like posers (such as the Prankquean's riddle)?" Perhaps more important is the apparent conflict between singular and plural verbs in "doe we aime," which means "do we am" as well as "do we aim" and "do we like" (French *aimer*); the paradox is resolved when we realize that Issy, who is sometimes one girl and sometimes two (when she is the two girls in the Park or when she is talking to her mirror image), is asking the question.

Viewed from this perspective, Issy's question centers on the mystery of her own split personality.

In a later chapter, during Shaun's story of the Ondt and the Gracehoper (414-19)—Shaun as the prudent ant and Shem as the wasteful grasshopper—there is yet another version of the Prankquean's riddle:

> The Gracehoper who, though blind as batflea, yet knew, not a leetle beetle, his good smetterling of entymology . . . promptly tossed himself in the vico . . . tezzily wondering wheer would his aluck alight or boss of both appease. . . . (417.3-7)

The Gracehoper's blindness contrasts with "his good smetterling of entymology": he knows something about insects (entomology) and word derivation (etymology), but apparently he has a thorough knowledge of neither. The insect-knowledge is knowledge of incest, since the Gracehoper was always trying (apparently unsuccessfully) to get various girls "to commence insects with him" (414.26-27); this sinful knowledge is equated with the knowledge of the origins of words, of the Word, of the world—in short, creation. Caught up in the Viconian cycle of life and death ("in the vico") in which everything changes, the Gracehoper seeks more knowledge of his relationship of the Ondt. The riddle, "wheer would his aluck alight or boss of both appease," may be rendered "where would he get lucky and appease his father, the 'boss' of both the boys"; more importantly, the riddle refers to the duality of apparent opposites (the "look-alike" theme again), and it asks about the reconciliation of the twins in the form of the "boss" or father figure.

Interestingly enough, "boss" is an amalgam of the Prankquean's "poss" and the "Bass" or Bass's Ale that Earwicker serves. This ale symbolizes the Trinity, partly because the label bears a red triangle, and it represents at the same time the union of the brothers ("both appease"= the two peas in the pod), who are "the basses brothers, those two theygottheres" (311.3-4). The "pea" or "pee" motif relates the ale to urine, so that "boss of both appease" may be glossed as "the sacramental ale created from the union of both the peas (twins)" or as "the sacramental ale created from urination (the peeing of the two girls in the Park)." The urination motif, then, connects this riddle to the Fall of Earwicker in the Park. If, as I believe, Bass's Ale represents the Trinitarian composite, the two interpretations I have just offered are paradoxical: while the first suggests that the Trinity (one from three) is created from the union of the brothers in, or with, their father, the second means that the Trinity (three from one) resulted from the Fall, which created Shem and Shaun and set them in opposition against each other and against their father. The paradox of order through disorder, which Joyce seems to be developing here, appears again in the next statement of the riddle.

When the motif of the Prankquean's riddle reappears in the interrogation of Yawn, the questioner is not clearly identified, although it can be assumed to be one of the Four Old Men. Clearly, however, the question is directed at Anna Livia. According to the *Skeleton Key*, Anna Livia appears under three aspects when she gives her testimony: first she is one of the girls in the Park, then the other, then the forgiving, mature wife.[37] As the first, darker girl she is the "raven" (491-93), while as the second, fairer girl she is the "dove" (493-94). The girls are both temptresses and victims of rape, and since in this chapter Earwicker is depicted as a British imperialist, the raven is India while the dove is Ireland—two countries that were exploited by the British. The riddle is posed at the juncture between Anna Livia's Indian and Irish stages, when one of the Four advises her to arise against oppression:

> —Let Eivin bemember for Gates of Gold for their fadeless suns berayed her. Irise, Osirises! Be thy mouth given unto thee! For why do you lack a link of luck to poise a pont of perfect, peace? (493.27-30)

"Eivin" or Anna Livia is Eve and Erin, betrayed by her faithless sons but also, paradoxically, illuminated by her unfading "suns"; as Issy, she is probably also Isis, sister-wife of Osiris

("Osirises"). The point seems to be that if Anna Livia's sons-brothers-husbands will arise and unite, they can attain the "perfect peace" that is now lacking. Alternately, the "fadeless suns" may be the proverbial sun which never sets on the British empire, and the riddle may ask "where is the missing link which by its absence imposes upon this perfect peace?" The "missing link" is presumably Ireland, which is called upon to disrupt the *pax Britanum*. Looking Januslike in two directions, the riddle inquires into the questions of "poise" (equilibrium, stability, interdependence of parts) and instability (the missing link in the chain of being or the British empire); the paradox of order and disorder, which was treated in theological terms in the last statement of the riddle, is here treated in political terms.

In the end the Prankquean's riddle is as mysterious as in the beginning. The final statement of the riddle comes during Anna Livia's parting monologue (621-28), in which she reminisces over the past and speculates about the future. She suggests a visit to the "Old Lord" whose "door is always open," warns her husband to be polite ("Remember to take off your white hat, ech?"), and promises to drop her "graciast kertssey" (623.4-11). Plainly enough, the Old Lord is God ("His is house of laws") and the passage, uttered by a river-woman who is about to die through absorption into the sea, looks forward to a meeting with God. He should be good to them, the woman contends: "You invoiced him last Eatster so he ought to give us hockockles and everything." Her "graciast kertssey," however, is more than a gracious curtsey (or a *deo gratias*), for Grace O'Malley and Kersse the Tailor are included in the phrase, and Anna Livia warns that if God does not treat them properly she will treat him as the Prankquean treated Jarl van Hoother:

> If the Ming Tung no go bo to me homage me hamage kow bow tow to the Mong Tang. Ceremonialness to stand lowest place be! Saying: What'll you take to link to light a pike on porpoise, plaise? He might knight you an Armor elsor daub you the first cheap magyerstrape. Remember Bomthomanew vim vam vom Hungerig. (623.11-17)

The visit of the Prankquean to van Hoother's castle, which is predicted here, is compared to a visit to heaven, with the Prankquean asking God to answer a riddle or tempting him with a bribe. The fish imagery in the riddle ("pike . . . porpoise, plaise") probably alludes to the traditional use of the fish as a symbol for Christ, and the question could therefore be read as an inquiry into the "link" between Christ's roles at two extremes of the chain of being—as the Light (John 1:5-9) and as the fish (symbolic of the sacramental food). The real question is whether these correspondences between spirit and flesh (Christ as the Light and Christ as fish) are established by design—"on porpoise"—or whether they are the result of chance. Although the answer is not given here, it seems fair to speculate that Joyce's answer would be that the intricate order of the world, like that of *Finnegans Wake,* derives partly from design and partly from coincidence.

In this final statement of the riddle, the Prankquean may be bribing God to reveal the secrets of his creation or she may be tempting him sexually: the pike or pikestaff is clearly phallic, and "to light a pike" may be glossed as "to arouse (light up) a penis" (cf. "And she lit up and fireland was ablaze"—21.16-17). The many standard meanings of the noun "pike"—pikestaff, turnpike, peaked summit, or a toll gate or the toll paid there—should serve to indicate the impossibility of an exhaustive interpretation of the riddle. It seems unlikely, for example, that Joyce missed the symbolic potential of the pike (toll gate) as the gateway to heaven, or the pike (toll) as the toll of death that must be paid before one passes into heaven, since the popular mind has instinctively made this connection.[38] In any case, the pike-toll as death, which stands in ironic contrast to the pike-fish as the Eucharist, is appropriate in the context of Anna Livia's impending death and rebirth. It seems likely, too, that the the "pike" is Norwegian *pike,* "girl," as in "Bauv Betty Famm and Pig Pig Pike" (420.10-11), in which both *pike* and its Danish cognate *pige* are present. If this meaning is intended, the theme of sexual temptation is clear: the Prankquean is brazenly propositioning God, asking for a sexual link between the Light and a *pike*. Virgin births, a rarity in the world, are excluded from *Finnegans Wake*.

The "why do I am alook alike a poss of porterpease" motif, complex enough from the beginning, becomes by the end of the book one of the most puzzling, yet one of the most meaningful, motifs in the *Wake*. By retaining the basic rhythm of the riddle while changing not only the words but even, at times, the major consonant sounds and the syntax, Joyce is able to adapt his riddle to almost any situation and—more importantly—any theme he desires. It is the rhythm of the sentence that establishes correspondences between parts of the book (e.g., the structural parallels between the stories of the Prankquean and the Norwegian Captain). The ultimate meaning of the riddle—like that of *Finnegans Wake* as a whole—will not and cannot be fully known and stated in plain terms, for the riddle is that of existence itself; the dreamer, who is both attracted and repelled by the mystery represented by the riddle, returns to it constantly, rephrasing it to make more sense of it but never penetrating its meaning.

6
Whose Hue: Izod's Heliotrope Riddle

A comparison of The Tale of Jarl van Hoother and The Mime of Mick, Nick and the Maggies (II.1) illustrates the way Joyce establishes a motif, then modifies and expands it in order to develop his thesis that all actions are "The seim anew" (215.23) and may be reduced to a few archetypal patterns. Many parallels establish the Mime as yet another reenactment of the temptation and the Fall of Man, this time presented as a play performed by Earwicker's children "Every evening at lighting up o'clock sharp" (219.1). Beginning with a playbill that includes a description of the cast, a list of credits, and an argument, the play is divided into three acts, each revolving around an attempt by Glugg (Shem) to answer the riddle posed by his sister, Izod (Issy). Among the parallels between the Mime and the Prankquean episode are the thunder-word at the end of the play (257.27-28); a number of allusions to the story of the Prankquean, including a parody of her riddle (224.14-15); the recurrence of the urination theme (225.6-7, 229.22-23); and the tripartite structure itself. But certain elements are reversed: it is Glugg who runs away between attempts to answer the riddle, and while van Hoother was clearly linked to the rainbow colors in the earlier story, Izod, the riddler, is the current representative of the spectrum. Here, even more explicitly than in The Tale of Jarl van Hoother, the riddle is combined with the folklore motif of the suitor test, for while van Hoother refuses

Whose Hue: Izod's Heliotrope Riddle

to try to guess the answer to the Prankquean's riddle, Glugg tries his best to find the answer to the Mime riddle because by doing so he will win Izod as his bride.[1] If the Prankquean's riddle is largely a question about identity and interrelationships among people, divinities, and pots of porter, the riddle posed here is again a question of "Who's who"—or, more exactly, "whose hue" (227.25), for Glugg's problem is to guess the color of his sister's drawers: "he must fand for himself by gazework what their colours wear as they are all showen drawens up" (224.26-27; cf. 233.9-10, 248.35-36). Sexual ability being explicitly compared to the ability to distinguish colors (248.21-22), Glugg's failure "to catch her by the calour of her brideness" (223.5-6) is a metaphor for his impotence.

Joyce described the basis of the Mime in a letter to Harriet Shaw Weaver dated 22 November 1930:

> The scheme of the piece I sent you is the game we used to call Angels and Devils or colours. The Angels, girls, are grouped behind the Angel, Shawn, and the Devil has to come over three times and ask for a colour. If the colour he asks for has been chosen by any girl she has to run and he tries to catch her. As far as I have written he has come twice and been twice baffled. The piece is full of rhythms taken from English singing games. When first baffled vindictively he thinks of publishing blackmail stuff about his father, mother etc etc etc. The second time he maunders off into sentimental poetry of what I actually wrote at the age of nine: 'My cot alas that dear old shady home where oft in youthful sport I played, upon thy verdant grassy fields all day or lingered for a moment in thy bosom shade etc etc etc etc.' This is interrupted by a violent pang of toothache after which he throws a fit. When he is baffled a second time the girl angels sing a hymn of liberation around Shawn. ... Note specially the treatment of the double rainbow in which the iritic colours are first normal and then reversed.[2]

In a letter written to Frank Budgen after the publication of *Finnegans Wake,* Joyce observed that the answer to Izod's riddle is "heliotrope."[3] This richly suggestive word, which literally means "turning toward the sun," may denote a color (soft, rosy purple), a stone (the bloodstone), or any of a number of plants. Although Joyce seems more interested in "heliotrope" as a color than as a plant or jewel, all three meanings are relevant: the Maggies (a multiple representation of Issy) are usually associated with plants or flowers, and in his first series of guesses (225.22-27) Glugg concentrates on stones—"monbreamstone" (moonstone, brimstone), "Hellfeuersteyn" (firestone or flint), and "Van Diemen's coral pearl" (Tasmanian pearl).

Whether seen as a stone, plant, or color, "heliotrope" appears frequently in the *Wake* and is often associated with the Park incident and the fall of the father. Kate's reaction to Earwicker's lame denial of guilt in the affair is summed up by her sneering comment "Hell o' your troop!" (273.24-25); Issy confesses to Jaun that she "always had a crush on heliotrope since the dusess of yore cycled round the Finest [Phoenix] Park" (461.8-10); one of the inquisitors demands of Yawn whether or not the cause of Earwicker's fatal attraction for girls was his "haliodraping het" (509.22); and Earwicker himself, testifying about the affair, admits that he loved to savor girls "served with heliotrope ayelips" (533.2). In Book IV, one of the directions for the silent film version of the "Park Mooting" that precedes the disputation between St. Patrick and the Archdruid is "Heliotrope leads from Harem" (610.36-611.1). Finally, since "heliotrope" is associated with the Park incident, which led to Earwicker's fall, it is appropriate that the merging of Butt and Taff into Buckley, who will shoot the Russian General, takes place in the *"heliotropical noughttime"* (349.6).

Appearing in the Mime as the answer to Izod's riddle, "heliotrope" serves a dual function: it reveals the strong connection between an apparently innocent children's game and Earwicker's guilty adventure in the Park, and it indicates Issy's preference for Shaun or Chuff, the sun-god who is worshipped by the "holytroopers." It seems to me, however, that Izod has her eye on her father as well as her brother, and that the Mime is in part her deliberate attempt to remind her father of his involvement in the nocturnal escapade in Phoenix Park and to arouse him sexually. Glugg, who lusts for his sister, unwittingly

Whose Hue: Izod's Heliotrope Riddle

plays Earwicker's part (Chuff acts out the part of the three soldiers who witnessed the incident), but while Earwicker failed with the girls in the Park because he was too old, Glugg fails because he is too young. Rejecting Glugg, Izod settles her attentions on Chuff who, as the son and the sun, represents a new generation and the promise of a new day that will see Earwicker deposed. But the new day has not yet risen; and since Glugg is impotent and Chuff is ignorantly Puritanical, Izod is still interested in arousing her father, the "Caesar-in-Chief" (219.13) who watches the game.

Unable to stand it any more, Earwicker arises (or is aroused) toward the end of the play and takes charge again. He has solved the riddle of his daughter's charade, and his desires are revealed by his "you-know-what-I've-come-about-I-saw-your-act air" (255.25). On the naturalistic level, the thunder near the end of the chapter is the sound of Earwicker slamming the door to his children's room, shutting his daughter in her room to avoid further temptation and to put an end to the parody of the Park incident (much as Jarl van Hoother attempted to shut the Prankquean out of his castle); within the framework of the play, the "thunder" is actually the fall of the curtain at the end of the third act, for it is followed by applause (257.30). At the same time, as Adaline Glasheen maintains, the sound of the thunder marks "a fall-creation for the father and an end to the daughter's barrenness" and recapitulates the fall of Jarl van Hoother.[4] This idea is carried over into the next chapter (the "studies" section), in which the textbook describes the creation of the Seven Wonders of the World from the mating of the "maker" (Earwicker as creator or father) and the "made" (Issy as the daughter-creation) (261.8-13).

Joyce combines the "Angels and Devils" theme of the children's game with the dramatic structure of the episode and turns the chapter into a parody of a morality play. Issy is presumably Everygirl deciding what path to take, while the boys play the parts of the good and bad angels who attempt to influence her decision. Chuff or Mick is Michael the Archangel:

"Chuffy was a nangel then and his soard fleshed light like likening. Fools top! Singty, sangty, meekly loose, defendy nous from prowlabouts. Make a shine on the curst. Emen" (222.22-24). Glugg or Nick is Satan: "But the duvlin sulph was in Glugger" who was "whipping his eyesoult and gnatsching his teats [cf. Matthew 25:30]" (222.25-27). The ultimate victory of Michael over Satan is recorded in a painting that hangs over the mantelpiece in Mr. and Mrs. Porter's bedroom (559.11-12), but in this episode their battle (252-53) is as inconclusive as the first two days of the battle between the rebels and the loyalists in Book VI of *Paradise Lost,* and the two boys fight "until they adumbrace a pattern of somebody else or other" (220.15-16). That "somebody else" is their father, the *deus ex machina* or "god of all machineries" (253.33) whose emergence puts a stop to the fighting.

Significantly, however, the two boys do not fight until Glugg has failed for the third time to solve Izod's riddle; prior to that, the conflict is the test of wits between Izod and Glugg, with saintly Chuff abstaining from active participation in the game. The humor of the episode derives from a simple reversal: Satanic Glugg is not the tempter but the tempted. While in the Bible and in *Paradise Lost* Satan tempts the woman to become godlike by eating the forbidden fruit, Joyce's version is that the woman tempts the "devil" to take over the role of the Father and to know both good and evil by tasting the fruit forbidden him by incest taboos. Simultaneously, Joyce parodies a familiar folklore motif, the contest of wits between a human being and the devil, with the human's soul at stake. Again there is a reversal: it is Glugg, not Izod, who has the most to lose in the game, for to Izod the question is not whether or not she will lose her virginity (that is taken for granted) but which male will take it. The symbolic treatment of the loss of virginity as the loss of one's soul, crucial to the allegorical interpretation of this episode as a suitor test, may be explained in part by reference to Joyce's notes on *Exiles:* "The soul like the body may have a virginity. For the woman to yield it or for the man to take it is the act of love."[5] The ambiguous treatment of the contest of wits in the Mime, with Glugg playing a dual role as demon and suitor, both strengthens and parodies Joyce's analogy between the body and the soul.

Glugg's failure in both roles is a metaphor for the impotence of a young boy who has not yet sexually matured, but there are a number of other reasons for his failure. Although he himself is a riddler, he lacks the wit required to solve his sister's riddle. It should be recalled that Stephen Dedalus was unable to solve Athy's riddle in the *Portrait,* and that even though Stephen posed highly symbolic riddles in *Ulysses* he did not even attempt to solve Lenehan's relatively simple conundrum. Glugg's lack of wit is amply displayed by his inability to decipher a number of charades and other clues that Margaret Solomon has explicated,[6] although it must be said in defense of Glugg that it is rather doubtful that most people would ever have solved these puzzles either. Izod, for one, views Glugg's failure as evidence that he is not too intelligent, or perhaps that he is inarticulate: "It's driving her dafft like he's so dumnb" (225.17-18).

A more serious defect, at least in a game that depends on the identification of colors, is Glugg's or Shem's poor vision, which is alluded to throughout the *Wake*—even Shem's writings are "strabismal" (189.8). The division of the father into his "semisized" sons leaves them both with sensory handicaps: Shaun apparently has clear vision but is hard of hearing, perhaps tone deaf, while Shem seems to share Joyce's acute ear for music and, unfortunately, his poor eyesight. Like Joyce, too, Shem is often seen with an eyepatch.[7] Glugg's visual problems are compounded by the dim light: the play began at "lighting up o'clock sharp," which seems to mean that it is late enough for the gas lamps to be lit, and Hart calculates that on the naturalistic level the Mime lasts from 8:30 to 9:00 P.M.[8] Furthermore, despite a number of clues—none of them very obvious—and the complaint about Glugg's stupidity, Izod does all she can to prevent her brother from getting a close look at the color of her (or her companions') underwear: "Angelinas, hide from light those hues that your sin beau may bring to light! Though down to your dowerstrip he's bent to knee he maun't know ledgings here" (233.5–7). All of this makes poor Glugg's "gazework" very difficult, of course, but he probably never had a chance anyway, for he seems (at least at this point) to be color-blind: "He knows for he's seen it in black and white through his eyetrompit trained upon jenny's and all that sort of thing which is dandymount to a clearobscure" (247.32–33).

One other interpretation of Glugg's failure is that it is due to his inability to spell—a metaphor for the inability to create or procreate. As a devil, Glugg attempts to work a kind of wordmagic by casting a spell over Izod, but he fails in this as in his attempt to spell "heliotrope": in II.2 Issy derides "Mr Tellibly Divilcult" or devilish Glugg, who was "not aebel ["not Abel" = Cain] to speel eelyotripes" (303.F1). Joyce extends the creative associations of the spelling motif (literary creation, wordmagic) to include "spilling" or urination, which is associated throughout the *Wake* with the flow of the River Liffey, Joyce's prime symbol for renewal and regeneration. The "spilling" of the temptresses in the Park, however, led to Earwicker's downfall, and Izod's "spelling" game now dooms Glugg. Given three anagrams for "heliotrope"—"O theoperil! Ethiaop lore, the poor lie" (223.28)—Glugg is unable to rearrange the letters, spell the answer, and win the girl. His failure stands in sharp contrast to the success of the girls in the Park, who "were white in black arpists at cloever spilling" (508.33). The phrase "white in black arpists" seems primarily to mean "literary artists," and indeed there is a clear parallel between what Shem the Penman does (or tries to do) and the "cloever spilling" of the girls: Shem first "spills" his urine and other bodily wastes, the raw products out of which he makes corrosive ink (27.9–11, 185.14–186.8), then "spells" with it, organizes it in intelligible patterns.[9] The process of spilling and spelling is disturbed by Izod and the Maggies in the Mime: Glugg's literary effort (231.5–8) is absurdly bad, and instead of creating corrosive ink out of his

Whose Hue: Izod's Heliotrope Riddle   143

urine, "he make peace in his preaches and play with esteem" (225.6-7), wetting his britches and playing with the steam (or "stem," urination giving way to fruitless masturbation).

Glugg's poor spelling aligns him with the forger Richard Pigott, whose misspelling of "hesitancy" doomed him (26.35, 97.25); completing the circle of allusions to spelling errors that precede a fall, Joyce connects Pigott's failure to keep his letters straight with Earwicker's failure to act properly—to "mind his P's and Q's"—when aroused by P and Q, the two girls in Phoenix Park (349.3, 350.17). The connection between spelling and the simultaneous fall and creation, it should be noted, does not depend merely upon the spilling/spelling pun that is the vehicle for Joyce's allegory: Adaline Glasheen comments that as early as the first chapter Joyce treats writing as "an act equivalent to eating of the tree of knowledge." In the "studies" chapter, she notes, "Issy knows her letters because she has eaten of the fruit, and she proves her knowledge when one part of her dissociated self . . . writes a mash note, thanking the professor who taught her to err (279.note 1); the other part of her personality writes a model letter, modeled on the letter from Boston, Mass. (280.1-281.3)."[10] Shem has the same knowledge: he is usually named as the author of the letter about his father, and as Dolph he explains the secrets of his mother's body to Kev or Shaun (293-99); but his possession of this knowledge combined with his inability to use it—his knowledge of the alphabet combined with his inability to spell—only serves to frustrate him.

The basic pattern of action in the Mime is fairly simple: Glugg is given three chances to guess the answer to the riddle (for each chance he takes three guesses), and each time he fails. After the first and second attempts the girls praise Chuff while Glugg runs away, and after the third attempt the boys fight, becoming virtually indistinguishable from each other so that the girls cannot tell "who is artthoudux from whose heterotropic" (252.20-21). Chaos leads to rebirth: the father emerges (253.29-32) and puts an end to the fighting. At the end of the chapter the children are in their room preparing to do their lessons before going to sleep.

While general patterns in the *Wake* are usually clear, however, specific details are more confusing. Joyce's use of "heliotrope" as the answer to the riddle is one such confusing detail. In the argument to the Mime, Glugg, stimulated by "those first girly stirs" (222.33), tries to guess the answer but cannot. The correct answer is "Not Rose, Sevilla nor Citronelle; not Esmeralde, Pervinca nor Indra; not Viola even" (223.6-7); it is none of the colors of the rainbow, all of which are included in this list, "nor all of them four themes over." Instead Izod— taking her identity from her color—is "all thees thing" (223.9). Izod is not playing fair: if her color were really a combination of "all thees thing" she would be white, not heliotrope. The Maggies or RAYNBOW girls (226.30-32) are formed by passing white Izod through a prism; the last rainbow color, violet, is virtually the same as heliotrope, but Joyce seems here to be looking for an idea rather than a color, and the correct answer is "not Viola even." It is the denotative significance of "heliotrope" that is really important, for Joyce's symbolism in the *Wake* is more often semantic than visual: all of the girls, whatever their colors, are "holytroopers" (223.11) or heliotropic worshipers of "Sunny" Chuff, and they are appropriately represented as a rainbow which, since it must face the sun, is by its very nature "heliotropic." Part of the significance of the Maggies derives from the fact that there are seven of them, for the number seven is associated with the fall of Jarl van Hoother, who wore seven articles of clothing and seven colors just before his defeat by the Prankquean; with God's creation of the world in seven days and man's creation of the Seven Wonders of the Ancient World; and with the seven sacraments of the Catholic Church, against which Glugg fights (227.29-228.2), as well as with the seven colors of the rainbow. One and seven, white light and the rainbow, unity and diversity are a constant theme in *Finnegans Wake:* Earwicker has his fling with a spectrum of girls but always returns to "fair" Anna Livia (215.19-22), while in Book IV (611–13) the Archdruid Berkeley (Shem) and St. Patrick (Shaun) argue the relative merits of the spectrum (associated with the fallen world and finiteness) and white light (associated with eternity).

One of the passages in the Mime argument that has caused some critical difficulty is an apparently simple pair of questions and answers: "A space. Who are you? The cat's mother. A time. What do you lack? The look of a queen" (233.23–24). Margaret Solomon believes that "It is not clear who asks the questions . . . and who gives the answers. Perhaps it is Glugg seeking clues and getting nowhere, or perhaps it is Chuff exercising a ritual of the game, getting wrong answers from Glugg."[11] The authors of the *Skeleton Key* translate the passage so that Glugg asks both questions and is answered by one of the girls (not necessarily Izod).[12] All of these possibilities must be admitted, but it is more likely that the terms "A space" and "A time" apply, respectively, to space-oriented Chuff and time-oriented Glugg, and that each of the brothers asks a question. Chuff is characteristically blunt ("Who are you?"), but the answer is evasive. Glugg tries a more subtle approach: "What do you lack?" he asks—remembering, perhaps, his success with his "when is a man not a man?" riddle, which centered on his father's deficiencies, or perhaps referring to Izod's lack of a penis. Izod's answer, "The look of a queen," indicates that she, like the Prankquean, is less queenlike than queanlike.

The problem, however, still remains: what do the answers have to do with "heliotrope"? As far as I know, no explanation of this problem has yet been published, but Janet Dunleavy has suggested to me that the passage parodies a children's guessing game in which the person who knows the answer is asked questions and must respond in such a way as to give a clue to the answer without actually giving it away. Here the two questions demand responses that are similar to "heliotrope" in "space" (length of the word) and "time" (rhythm of the word). Izod's clues are appropriate: disregarding initial articles, we note that "cat's mother," like "heliotrope," has ten letters, while the rhythm of "lóok ŏf ă quéen" is essentially that of "hĕ-lĭ-ŏ-trópe." The clues, however, are too subtle for the boys, and while this does not seem to bother Chuff, Glugg searches the four elements (each identified with one of the evangelists) for the answer (223.29-33). They can't help him—he doesn't even get a wire from the ether (223.34)—so he goes into exile.

A certain amount of confusion has been generated by the Mime riddles and their answers. Even Bernard Benstock's usually reliable "Working Outline of *Finnegans Wake*" includes several questionable readings: Benstock indicates that on pages 224-25 "Glugg asked [is asked] the first riddle—about jewels—loses"; on page 233 "Glugg asked the second riddle—on insects—loses again"; and on page 250 "Glugg asked the third riddle—loses again."[13] Actually the first riddle is not "asked" at all but, being an integral part of the Angels and Devils game which the children are playing, is already in Glugg's mind: the "boy fiend" Glugg "cometh up as a trapadour, sinking how he must fand for himself by gazework what their colours wear as they are all showen drawens up" (224.25-27). The Satanic motif here is important: not only a troubadour, Glugg is a "fiend" who emerges through a trapdoor (spelled "dour," in part to remind us of the "dour" van Hoother), and he wonders how the devil he can "fand" (Danish *Fanden,* the Devil) the answer. Glugg's demonic disposition colors his first set of answers, which includes puns on brimstone ("monbreamstone"), hellfire ("Hellfeuersteyn"), and demon ("Van Diemen's coral pearl") (225.22-26). The *riddle* is not "about jewels" at all, and although the first and third answers include references to jewels—moonstone and pearl—the only stone I can see in the second answer is firestone (German *Feuerstein*), which is not a jewel. A more significant factor is the use of hell-fire and brimstone to describe the fires of passion that consume the demonic lover, Glugg.

The second time the riddle appears, it is altered: "Find the frenge for frocks and translace it into shocks of such as touch with show and show" (233.9-10). Here, the task of discovering the color of the "fringe" worn by the girls is confused with an assignment in French translation, which is probably why French *jaune* (yellow) finds its way into the next two answers, "jaoneofergs" and "mayjaunties." Epstein sees yellow in the third answer, "nunsibellies," too, relying for this identification on Joyce's reference (in a letter to Italo Svevo) to an elastic band "the colour of a nun's belly."[14] Epstein points out more French in the answers: "'jaoneofergs' = Joan of Arc, 'mayjaunties' = *mes gentils,* 'nunsibellies' = *non si belles.*"[15] It might be added that "show" (in the riddle statement) puns on French *chaud* (heat, warmth), while the first two answers in this set offer puns on *jeunes vierges* (young virgins) and *mes jeunes filles* (my girls). Besides Joan of Arc, the names of other girls are hidden in the answers: Jennifers—perhaps related to the "jinnies" who plague "willingdone"—in "jaoneofergs"; May (and possibly June) in "mayjaunties"; Nancy, Bella, and Ellie in "nunsibellies." The last answer, punning both on Italian *belle* (sweethearts) and Latin *belli* (of war), is an appropriate description of the "maggies" who make love into a battle: "They war loving" (142.31).[16]

This does not, however, get us any closer to the insects that Benstock finds in the passage. Benstock apparently trusted the judgment of the *Skeleton Key,* which states that "Glugg appears to be guessing in terms of colored insects and fishing flies, lures of the love-angler."[17] This is an appealing idea, especially since references to insects are often disguises for incestuous desires (e.g., at 414.26-27), but the glosses on Glugg's answers offered by the authors of the *Skeleton Key* are not very convincing. Campbell and Robinson substitute "speckled Fergusons" for "jaoneofergs," "yellow May flies" for "mayjaunties," and "pretty little nun-moths" for "nunsibellies." The "yellow May flies" appear reasonable (even though none of the mayflies I have ever seen were yellow) since both May and yellow *(jaune)* are obviously part of the answer, but the other two translations cannot easily be substantiated and seem to me more like ingenious attempts to discern an "insectuous" pattern in the answers than defensible glosses. Epstein, who first says that these three answers "all seem to refer to insects" and then partly retracts that judgment in a footnote, offers June bugs and libellules or dragonflies as glosses on the first and third answers while sticking with mayflies for "mayjaunties."[18] Whatever critics of *Finnegans Wake* search for they are certain to find, but surely the evidence that Glugg's guesses refer primarily to insects has yet to be conclusively demonstrated.

The third set of answers (250.3-9) is even more complex than the first two. Again the problem is set before Glugg: "Radouga, Rab will ye na pick them in their pink of panties" (248.35-36). The guesses come after a number of clues and a dance in which the girls "point in the shem direction as if to shun" (249.28), an indication that as darkness falls the twins are beginning to be indistinguishable. Margaret Solomon says that "it is not clear whether Glugg makes the last three guesses or whether Izod makes them for him while he 'speaks' with gestures,"[19] but in either case this set of answers is Glugg's last chance to win Izod. A certain amount of internal evidence points to Glugg as the speaker: earlier he saw a "sight most deletious to ross up the spyballs" (247.20-21), and "ross" is echoed in his first guess: "Willest thou rossy banders havind?" (250.3). Several interpretations are possible: "Do you have a rosy band?"; "Would you like a vicious [French *rosse*] bandaging [French *bander* = to bandage]?"; "Would you like to be thrashed [French *rosser* = to thrash] and bound?"; "What will you have, gypsy woman [Gaelic *rasaidhe*]?" Campbell and Robinson, who assume that Izod asks the question, pick up echoes of French *rosser* and German *Ross* (steed) and translate the passage "Would you like to be tamed by some little horse-breakers?"[20] Acting out the question, Glugg "simules to be tight in ribbings round his rumpffkorpff," then tries again: "Are you Swarthants that's hit on a shorn stile?" The *Skeleton Key* translates this as "Are you Blackhands, the chimneysweep?" The accuracy of this interpretation—which would seem to indicate that the question is directed at Glugg—is borne out by Glugg's pantomime ("He makes semblant to be swiping their chimbleys") and by the pun on German *Schornstein,* "chimney." But the "shorn stile" is also a dagger (Italian *stile*) and a fountain pen (French *stylo*), and "Swarthants" is also Schwarzer Hans, whom Helmut Bonheim identifies as a devil figure.[21] If the "stile" is a phallic image (as pens usually are in the *Wake*), then Izod could be asking "Are you the poor devil with the worn-out (castrated) penis?" If the question is asked by Glugg, he could be asking "Are you the swarthy aunts (or ants) who are stuck on Chuff's shorn (circumcised?) penis?"

Glugg comes closest to his real desires in the last question and charade: he asks "Can you ajew ajew fro' Sheidam?" and he "finges to be cutting up with a pair of sissers [scissors, sisters] and to be buytings of their maidens and spitting their heads into their facepails." His interest is, after all, sexual: he wants to cut up with his sisters and to bite off their maidenheads. The translation of the question offered by the *Skeleton Key* is "Can you tell the difference between goodbye and divorce?" (French *adieu* = good-bye, German *scheiden* = to divorce). Izod may be asking Glugg to remove his sheath (to say *adieu* to the *Scheide,* German for "sheath") and to exhibit his penis, but it seems more likely that Glugg is posing the question and asking her to have sexual relations with him. This interpretation is supported by the apparent allusion to Joyce's own poem, Number XI in *Chamber Music,* which begins "Bid adieu, adieu, adieu,/ Bid adieu to girlish days."[22]

The complexity of Glugg's answers makes it difficult to find in them any clear pattern of development, but a pattern of sorts does emerge. In his first set of answers Glugg concentrates on stones and hell-fire, ending with a reference to Tasmania or van Diemen's Land. Glugg is looking downward—toward hell or the southern hemisphere—and his attitude is directly counterposed to the "heliotropic" posture adopted by Izod and her multiple incarnations, who raise their eyes to the sun-god Chuff and follow his horizontal orbit around the earth. (The word "sinking" and the pun on Gaelic *fanaidh*— sloping downward—in the statement of the problem [224.26] reinforce

Glugg's downcast attitude.) In his second set of answers Glugg, pretending to be "ernest" (233.20) like the characters in Wilde's play, tries to be more sophisticated and concentrates on French words and puns on girls' names. Yellow or *jaune* pervades these answers, perhaps because, as Epstein puts it, "Glugg's view is jaundiced because he is jealous of Chuff's ability to attract the Maggies,"[23] or on the other hand because Glugg is attempting to act "jaunty" and casual after his "jauntings" (225.34). More importantly, the color yellow is closely associated with the trial of Oscar Wilde:

> When headlines reported that Wilde, the arch transgressor, was seen reading a yellow book, angry citizens proceeded to stone the windows of the offices of *The Yellow Book,* an *avante garde* publication of the time. Actually Wilde's yellow book, *a* yellow book, was a French publication having nothing to do with the magazine. It was *Aphrodite* by Pierre Louys. Yellow was the "theme" color of the '90's, symbolizing the bizarre and the modern.[24]

Like Lynch, a character in *A Portrait of the Artist* and *Ulysses* whose "proof of . . . culture" was that he swore in yellow (*P* 204, *U* 433), Glugg seems to be imitating the followers of the Decadent movement.

In both of the first two sets of answers, however, Chuff or Shaun is also present: he is frequently represented as a stone, and he is probably alluded to in references to *jaune* not only because as "Sunny" he is associated with the yellow sun, but also because in III.2 he is known as Jaun. In the third set of answers Glugg is desperate and abandons the actual task at hand, the guessing of a color (although red and black are part of the first two answers); attempting to subvert the rules of the game and to win Izod by any possible means, he turns his "guesses" into a series of sexually suggestive questions.

The broader pattern of development is somewhat clearer. Like the tripartite structure of the Prankquean episode, the division of the Mime into three sections, each revolving around an attempt to answer the riddle, suggests a correspondence between the episode and the mythic pattern of three tasks or three attempts to complete a task. The feat is too great for immature Glugg, whose time has not yet come, so all three attempts end in failure. The three parts of the episode should also correspond to the ages of a Viconian cycle, although the complexity of the chapter is such that correspondences to any of the Viconian ages may be found on virtually any page. But the overall pattern follows the Viconian model: failure on the three attempts to answer the riddle (three Viconian ages) leads to chaos *(ricorso)*, which is resolved by the reemergence of the Father-God who ends the cycle and begins a new one by reasserting his authority and frightening the children with his thunder. The use of the Viconian superstructure universalizes the action, then, and expands the significance of Glugg's failure: Izod is Helen of Troy (248.11), Iseult, and all the other temptresses over whom men fight, and she will be taken when—and by whom—she pleases.

The Mime chapter begins what Tindall calls "the densest part of the *Wake*," the ninth, tenth, and eleventh chapters.[25] Here, with the middle of the dream approaching and the light fading outside, there is more obscurity than usual: even the basic narrative situation is partly in the dark, although there is little doubt that Izod either poses or embodies the riddle and that Glugg tries to guess it. The general murkiness of II.1 is likely to be an annoyance if we demand clarity and certainty, but when we experience the episode as a maze of conflicting patterns in the mind of the dreamer, we can see that the contradictions and uncertainties of the chapter are necessary aspects of its complex and riddlelike function. By the time Glugg makes his third attempt to answer the riddle, the scene is so dark that it is not absolutely clear whether Glugg or Izod is the speaker, and immediately thereafter the boys become indistinguishable or interchangeable, just as Jarl van Hoother's twins can exchange roles. In one important sense, then, the Mime is very much like the Park incident: the more we know about the event, the less we can be certain exactly who did what to whom and under what circumstances. What is clear, though, aside from the broad structural pattern of the chapter, is that our own uncertainty about what happens, like Glugg's failure to solve the riddle, is a commentary on the problem of knowledge and certainty in the "real" world and its dream reflection, where "the unfacts, did we possess them, are too imprecisely few to warrant our certitude" (57.16-17). In this way, the heliotrope episode is one of Joyce's many models for his "clearobscure" dream book.

Conclusion

The four decades that have passed since the completed text of *Finnegans Wake* was first unveiled have seen many advances in our understanding of this imposing book. Critics have discussed characterization, structure, narrative technique, literary allusions, foreign language elements, and a host of special topics ranging from Irish politics to Egyptian mythology.[1] Yet as Benstock has noted in a summary of *Finnegans Wake* scholarship, it is clear that while investigations of *Ulysses* promise "real solutions," studies of the *Wake* generally lead to "new frustrations."[2] Even so, these frustrations exist largely because many of our expectations have been exaggerated: as the hope of finding a skeleton key or Rosetta stone to unlock the book's mysteries fades, so will many of the disappointments that attend the failure of a new approach or a new collection of facts to account for more than a small part of the book.

My description of *Finnegans Wake* as a riddle is no doubt inadequate, but it does point to a significant element of Joyce's vision of his art. Again and again Joyce returns to the idea that the artist is a riddler, a constructor of verbal mazes where the reader finds himself "lost in the bush" without "the poultriest notions what the farest he all means" (122.3-6). The reader's difficulties in grappling with the text are reflected in the dreamer's struggle to free himself from the confusion and uncertainty of the dream world, and they are objectified in the recurrent attempts to decipher the "unreadable" text of Shem's letter. The description of Shem as a riddler, then, is simply another version of Joyce's determination to lose the reader in the bush. Yet the process of being lost in this "puling sample jungle of woods" is the real point of the book; that is, there is no lesson or central truth to be abstracted from the experience, only the experience itself. Indeed, while he poses as a figure of great learning, the artist has no truth to teach us except whatever is contained in the fruitless search for absolutes, for definitive solutions. As Margot Norris says, "The artist enjoys no corner on truth; he merely constructs more elaborate and elegant myths and lies more convincingly than the man on the street."[3] For this reason, perhaps, Joyce depicts the artist failing to answer others' riddles just as often as he shows the artist posing his own enigmas.

That *Finnegans Wake* can only be experienced—that it cannot be paraphrased or summarized to anyone's satisfaction—is one of its many riddlelike qualities. Yet this is a very odd and special sort of riddle, for most riddles are, ultimately, capable of being answered, if only by the riddler himself. *Finnegans Wake* cannot be "answered," defined in terms of its subject and meaning, for as Samuel Beckett noted the *Wake* "is not *about* something; *it is that something itself.*"[4] Joyce wanted his works to remain enigmatic: he told Jacques Benoîst-Méchin that in writing *Ulysses* he had "put in so many enigmas and puzzles that it will keep the professors busy for centuries."[5] Aside from providing even more material for professors to write about, the many puzzles of *Finnegans Wake* are an indication that Joyce took the conditions of his dream world seriously. Norris observes that

> The great problem, of course, is that the reader is trapped inside the dream in *Finnegans Wake*. A dream can't be analyzed from the inside, because the dream is precisely the place where self-knowledge breaks down. The dreamer confronts a disguised message from his own unconscious. He is unable to know his unconscious directly, and yet it is utterly and truly himself. The confusion of the reader of *Finnegans Wake* is a fitting response to a kind of terror implicit in the world of the dream.[6]

The very insolubility of the riddles, then, becomes a clue to their solution—if this perspective can be called a "solution." As an artist, Joyce imitates God, the prime maker of riddles and mysteries:

> What was after the universe? Nothing. But was there anything round the universe to show where it stopped before the nothing place began? It could not be a wall but there could be a thin thin line there all round everything. It was very big to think about everything and everywhere. Only God could do that. He tried to think what a big thought that must be but he could think only of God. (*P* 16)

Stephen's puzzlings over theological enigmas become more sophisticated (if often rather blasphemous) in *Ulysses,* but his inability to solve such puzzles as the consubstantiality of Father and Son (*U* 38) is simply another example of the ultimate inability of the finite, human mind to deal adequately with certain topics. Bloom, more practical-minded, has spent time wondering how to square the circle in order to win a million pounds in a puzzle contest (*U* 515, 699, 718), but has never come close to a solution. Even the apparently godlike narrator of "Ithaca" makes simple mistakes, as for instance when he claims that Bloom returned Stephen's money "without interest" (*U* 695) even though Bloom actually returned one penny more than he took from Stephen. Such errors in *Ulysses* are further examples of the fragmented surface of the novel, as Joyce constantly sets up his pose of omniscience and then betrays that pose with an error, volitional or not.

And *Finnegans Wake*? Here, where a simple and repeated call for the time of day (which usually doubles with the closing of the pub: "Time, please") is rarely given a straight answer, there seems little chance that the book's mysteries will all be solved. The way the book resists simplistic analysis and refuses its readers easy access into its center has alienated many who lack the patience that Joyce so often asks us to show: "Now, patience; and remember patience is the great thing, and above all things else we must avoid anything like being or becoming out of patience" (108.8-11). Yet those who have put enough effort into the *Finnegans Wake* experience to realize that the book "is not a miseffectual whyacinthinous riot of blots and blurs and bars and balls and hoops and wriggles and juxtaposed jottings linked by spurts of speed" are asked to "cling to it as with drowning hands" (118.28-30, 119.3). Joyce certainly clung to it even when many of his friends expressed grave doubts about *Work in Progress:* when Mary Colum said that his new work was "outside literature," he told her husband to "Tell her it may be outside literature now, but its future is inside literature."[7] *Finnegans Wake* is "inside literature" now, and it needs no further defense against those who condemn the *Wake* because they refuse to see it in its own terms; what we need, more than ever, is to debate exactly what those terms are. If this book has contributed something of value to that debate, it has achieved its purpose.

Notes

Chapter 1: The Riddle and Finnegans Wake

1. *Letters*, I, 213.
2. *Letters*, I, 251.
3. Herbert Howarth, *The Irish Writers 1880–1940* (London: Rockliff, 1958), p. 277; Wells, letter to Joyce in *Letters*, I, 275; Joseph Campbell and Henry Morton Robinson, *A Skeleton Key to Finnegans Wake* (New York: Viking Compass Edition, 1961), p. 3.
4. Frank Budgen, *James Joyce and the Making of Ulysses* (Bloomington: Indiana University Press, 1960), pp. 19–20. The final version of the sentences reads "Perfume of embraces all him assailed. With hungered flesh obscurely, he mutely craved to adore" (*U* 168).
5. *Letters*, I, 175; cf. *U* 668–69.
6. Budgen, p. 284.
7. *Poetics* 22, in *On Poetry and Style*, trans. G. M. A. Grube (Indianapolis: Library of Liberal Arts, 1958), p. 47. In the *Rhetoric* (3, ch. 2), Aristotle refers to this as a "well-known riddle" that describes "the process of cupping" (p. 71).
8. Archer Taylor, *English Riddles from Oral Tradition* (Berkeley: University of California Press, 1951), p. 1.
9. For a brief analysis of the Sphinx's riddle and English analogues see Taylor, *English Riddles*, pp. 20–24. For two Irish analogues see Vernam Hull and Archer Taylor, *A Collection of Irish Riddles* (Berkeley: University of California Press, 1955), p. 2.
10. The day-lifetime metaphor seems to be a later embellishment on a simpler version of the riddle such as the one Robert Graves cites: "What being, with only one voice, has sometimes two feet, sometimes three, sometimes four, and is weakest when it has most?" *The Greek Myths*, rev. ed. (Baltimore: Penguin Books, 1960), II, 10.
11. Cf. Taylor, *English Riddles*, p. 1.
12. This is the answer given in *Huckleberry Finn* (ch. 17). Frederic Peachy gives an alternate answer: "Under the bed, looking for his slippers (alias, *le pot de chambre* ...)." Introduction to *Clareti Enigmata: The Latin Riddles of Claret* (Berkeley: University of California Press, 1957), p. 3.

13. For further notes on Joyce's use of this riddle see Bernard Benstock, *Joyce-again's Wake* (Seattle: University of Washington Press, 1965), pp. 209–11, and Ward Swinson, "Riddles in *Finnegans Wake*," *Twentieth Century Literature* 19 (July 1973): 170.

14. Taylor, *English Riddles*, p. 1; cf. Hull and Taylor, pp. 65–66.

15. Whitley Stokes, "Irish Riddles," *Celtic Review* 1 (1904): 132–35; Hull and Taylor, pp. 73–74.

16. Vivian Mercier, *The Irish Comic Tradition* (Oxford: Oxford University Press, 1962), p. 81.

17. Weldon Thornton, *Allusions in Ulysses* (Chapel Hill: University of North Carolina Press, 1968), p. 26. M. J. MacManus, in *Eamon de Valera* (Dublin: Talbot Press, 1944), p. 137, gives a version that is closer to Stephen's than any cited by Thornton: "'Beware of the hoof of the horse, the horn of the bull and the smile of the Saxon.' —*Old Irish proverb*."

18. Taylor, *English Riddles*, pp. 267–71.

19. For exhaustive listings of allusions see Adaline Glasheen, *A Third Census of Finnegans Wake* (Berkeley: University of California Press, 1977), p. 133, and Mabel P. Worthington, "Nursery Rhymes in *Finnegans Wake*," *Journal of American Folklore* 70 (January–March 1957): 43–44.

20. See Adaline Glasheen, "Part of What the Thunder Said in *Finnegans Wake*," *Analyst*, no. 23 (November 1964), pp. 1–29; cf. Petr Skrabanek, "Structure and Motif in Thunderwords: A Proposal," *A Wake Newslitter* 12 (December 1975): 108–11.

21. Taylor, *English Riddles*, pp. 267–68.

22. Campbell and Robinson, p. 5.

23. See Taylor, *English Riddles*, pp. 301–3.

24. Vivian Mercier, "In the Wake of the Fianna," in *A James Joyce Miscellany, Third Series*, ed. Marvin Magalaner (Carbondale: Southern Illinois Univeristy Press, 1962), p. 236.

25. *"Dum moritur, generat semper. Granum tibi solvat."* ("What dies, and always gives birth?—A seed.") Peachy, p. 33; the source of the riddle, as Peachy observes, is probably John 12:34.

26. Peachy, p. 41.

27. Swinson, pp. 166–67.

28. Swinson, p. 167.

29. Johan Huizinga, *Homo Ludens: A Study of the Play-Element in Culture* (New York: Roy Publishers, 1950), p. 105. Similarly, Roger D. Abrahams notes that "Riddles are devices which are used to demonstrate control over words and objects and ideas that are central to the life of the riddling group." "The Literary Study of the Riddle," *Texas Studies in Literature and Language* 14 (Spring 1972): 182.

30. Fred Norris Robinson, *Satirists and Enchanters in Early Irish Literature* (American Committee for Irish Studies: Reprints in Irish Studies, no. 1, n.d.), pp. 125–27.

31. Archer Taylor, *The Literary Riddle Before 1600* (Berkeley: University of California Press, 1948), pp. 38–39.

32. See Stith Thompson, *Motif-Index of Folk-Literature*, rev. ed. (Bloomington: Indiana University Press, 1966), III, 398–449, and Tom Peete Cross, *Motif-Index of Early Irish Literature* (Bloomington: Indiana University Press, 1952), pp. 337–42. See especially Thompson, entries H507.1, H507.1.1, H508.2, H511, H551, H551.1, H551.2, H552, and Cross, entries H508.2 and H552.

Notes

33. For folklore analogues see Thompson, entry H511.1.

34. Mercier, *The Irish Comic Tradition,* p. 82; cf. Tom Peete Cross and Clark Harris Slover, *Ancient Irish Tales* (New York: Barnes & Noble, 1969), pp. 157-58.

35. Anthony Burgess, "If Oedipus Had Read His Lévi-Strauss," in *Urgent Copy* (New York: Norton, 1968), pp. 260-61.

36. Claude Lévi-Strauss, *The Scope of Anthropology,* trans. Sherry Ortner Paul and Robert A. Paul (London: Jonathan Cape, 1967), pp. 38-39.

37. See William York Tindall, "James Joyce and the Hermetic Tradition," *Journal of the History of Ideas* 15 (January 1954): 23-39.

38. Mercier, *The Irish Comic Tradition,* pp. 81-83.

39. Huizinga, p. 133.

40. Huizinga, p. 135.

41. Henry Frank Beechhold, "Early Irish History and Mythology in *Finnegans Wake*" (Ann Arbor: University Microfilms, 1956), pp. 2-3. The *fili* was a poet or seer, a man of great learning; see Mercier, *The Irish Comic Tradition,* passim, and Robin Flower, *The Irish Tradition* (Oxford: Oxford University Press, 1947), p. 4. The *ollave* spent seven years in a bardic school before seeking service as official poet to a king or chieftain (Flower, pp. 98-99).

42. Mercier, *The Irish Comic Tradition,* pp. 80-81.

43. Taylor, *The Literary Riddle,* pp. 6-7.

44. William York Tindall, *A Reader's Guide to James Joyce* (New York: Farrar, Straus and Giroux, 1959), p. 237.

45. Adaline Glasheen, *A Second Census of Finnegans Wake* (Evanston: Northwestern University Press, 1963), p. xvii.

46. Richard Ellmann, *James Joyce* (New York: Oxford University Press, 1959), p. 720.

47. *Letters,* I, 228.

Chapter 2: The Ulysses *Riddles*

1. William York Tindall, *A Reader's Guide to James Joyce* (New York: Farrar, Straus and Giroux, 1959), p. 13.

2. Roger D. Abrahams, "The Literary Study of the Riddle," *Texas Studies in Literature and Language* 14 (Spring 1972): 193. A version with a different answer is "John had a long thing. Mary had a hairy thing. John stuck his long thing in Mary's hairy thing. — a hug (hog) named Mary. John had a knife, 'n' he stuck it in de hog." Cited by Waln K. Brown, "Cognitive Ambiguity and the 'Pretended Obscene Riddle,'" *Keystone Folklore Quarterly* 18 (1973): 98.

3. Weldon Thornton, *Allusions in Ulysses* (Chapel Hill: University of North Carolina Press, 1968), p. 30. Ward Swinson, in "Riddles in *Finnegans Wake,*" *Twentieth Century Literature* 19 (July 1973): 168, cites another version.

4. Archer Taylor, *English Riddles from Oral Tradition* (Berkeley: University of California Press, 1951), pp. 435-39.

5. Taylor, pp. 435, 436.

6. Ovid, *Metamorphoses,* trans. Mary M. Innes (Baltimore: Penguin Books, 1955), pp. 37-40.

7. Adaline Glasheen, *A Third Census of Finnegans Wake* (Berkeley: University of California Press, 1977), p. 73.

8. Roy Arthur Swanson, "Edible Wandering Rocks: The Pun as Allegory in Joyce's 'Lestrygonians,'" *Genre*, 5 (December 1972): 396.

9. Thornton, pp. 30–31.

10. Alan Dundes, "The Study of Folklore in Literature and Culture: Identification and Interpretation," *Journal of American Folklore* 78 (April–June 1965): 137–38. (My thanks to Professor Alan M. Cohn for calling my attention to this article.) P. J. McCall cites a similar riddle and suggests as a possible answer "a soldier burying his sweetheart." "Folk Lore Riddles—Irish and Anglo-Irish," *Journal of the National Literary Society of Ireland* 1:2 (1900): 71–72.

11. Thornton, p. 473. For analogous genealogical riddles see Vernam Hull and Archer Taylor, *A Collection of Irish Riddles* (Berkeley: University of California Press, 1955), pp. 78–81.

12. William M. Schutte, *Joyce and Shakespeare* (New Haven: Yale University Press, 1957), pp. 107–8.

13. Schutte, p. 109; cf. Stuart Gilbert, *James Joyce's Ulysses*, new ed. (New York: Vintage Books, 1952), p. 106.

14. My point is further illustrated by Elaine Unkeless's observation that May Dedalus is portrayed as a vampire lover. "Bats and Sanguivorous Bugaboos," *James Joyce Quarterly* 15 (Winter 1978): 130–32.

15. For further commentary on the connection between the opera and the Blooms, see Zack Bowen, *Musical Allusions in the Works of James Joyce* (Albany: State University of New York Press, 1974), pp. 123–24, 166–67, 272–73.

16. On "The Last Rose of Summer," see Bowen, pp. 204–5, 333–34.

17. *Romeo and Juliet*, II.ii.43–44. As I noted in "Allusions in *Ulysses*: Random Addenda and Corrigenda for Thornton," *James Joyce Quarterly* 13 (Fall 1975): 56–57, the Shakespearean allusion is confirmed at *U* 622–23 when Stephen says "Shakespeares were as common as Murphies. What's in a name?" and Bloom replies "Yes, to be sure. . . . Of course. Our name [Virag] was changed too."

Chapter 3: *This Nightly Quisquiquock of the Twelve Apostrophes: The Quiz Chapter of* Finnegans Wake

1. On one level this riddle describes the fall of HCE: "shoots off in a hiss" = HCE's sin, involving urination or masturbation; "muddles up in a mussmass" = confusion (Earwicker's stuttering) and death; "his whole's a dismantled noondrunkard's son" = HCE's dismemberment (358.32–36) and replacement by his son. On another level, as Bernard Benstock has pointed out to me, the three parts of the riddle describe the procreative process of ejaculation, foetal development, and birth. Cf. Margaret C. Solomon, *Eternal Geomater* (Carbondale: Southern Illinois University Press, 1969), pp. 67–68.

2. The "four of them" are both the four questions (4, 6, 10, 12) that are answered by other people and the Four Old Men, who answer the fourth question. In III.4 the Four are the bedposts around Mr. and Mrs. Porter's bed; here they are the bearers of Shaun's "ripostes" to Shem's fourth question.

3. Hugh Kenner, *Dublin's Joyce* (Bloomington: Indiana University Press, 1956), p.1.

Notes 161

4. Cf. Adaline Glasheen, "Notes Towards a Supreme Understanding of the Use of 'Finnegan's Wake' in *Finnegans Wake*," *A Wake Newslitter* 5 (February 1968) :7.

5. William York Tindall, *A Reader's Guide to Finnegans Wake* (New York: Farrar, Straus and Giroux, 1969), p. 126. For more extensive commentaries, see Thomas A. Cowan, "Sacer Esto?", *A Wake Newslitter* 11 (June 1974): 39-44, and E. L. Epstein, "The Turning Point," in *A Conceptual Guide to Finnegans Wake*, ed. Michael H. Begnal and Fritz Senn (University Park: Pennsylvania State University Press, 1974), pp. 64-67.

6. *The New Science of Giambattista Vico*, Abridged Translation of the Third Edition (1744), trans. and ed. Thomas Goddard Bergin and Max Harold Fisch (Ithaca: Cornell University Press, 1970).

7. Clive Hart and Fritz Senn, "EXPLICATIONS—for the greeter glossary of code," *A Wake Newslitter*, o.s. no. 1 (March 1962), pp. 3-5.

8. Clive Hart has observed that the men in questions 1, 5, and 9 correspond to the Earwickers of Book I (man at the height of his powers), Book II (man on the decline), and Book III ("the ritually murdered Earwicker falling asleep"). *Structure and Motif in Finnegans Wake* (Evanston: Northwestern University Press, 1962), pp. 81-82.

9. Joseph Campbell and Henry Morton Robinson, *A Skeleton Key to Finnegans Wake* (New York: Viking Compass Edition, 1961), p. 108.

10. The tree (symbolic of Shem and St. Paul) and stone (Shaun and St. Peter) represent the brothers at the point of greatest division but promise renewal: united, tree and stone become tree-stone or Tristan, successor to HCE or King Mark. Grace Eckley analyzes the tree and stone images in detail in "Queer Mrs Quickenough and Odd Miss Doddpebble," in Michael H. Begnal and Grace Eckley, *Narrator and Character in Finnegans Wake* (Lewisburg, Pa.: Bucknell University Press, 1975).

11. Since Earwicker is the "Caesar-in-Chief" (219.13), Antonius is his successor. Brutus (Shaun) and Cassius (Shem) unite as Antony and replace Caesar as the lover of Cleopatra (Issy). See Bernard Benstock, *Joyce-again's Wake* (Seattle: University of Washington Press, 1965), pp. 26-28, and Roland McHugh, *The Sigla of Finnegans Wake* (Austin: University of Texas Press, 1976), p. 92.

12. Benstock, *Joyce-again's Wake*, pp. 189-90.

13. *A First-Draft Version of Finnegans Wake*, ed. David Hayman (London: Faber and Faber, 1963), pp. 27, 92-93.

14. Hart, pp. 179-80.

15. These symbols are reproduced in Hayman, pp. 92-98. The symbol for question 12 would be Shem's symbol, ⊏. Cf. McHugh, p. 32.

16. *Letters*, I, 213.

17. *Letters*, I, 250, 254.

18. A. Walton Litz, *The Art of James Joyce*, corrected edition (New York: Oxford University Press, 1964), pp. 116-17.

19. Henry F. Beechhold "Finn MacCool and *Finnegans Wake*," *James Joyce Review* 2 (Spring-Summer 1958): 10.

20. James S. Atherton, *The Books at the Wake* (New York: Viking Press, 1960), p. 268.

21. A phrase in the riddle identifies HCE with four other English Kings: "woollem the farsed, hahnreich the althe, charge the sackend, writchad the thord" (138.32-33).

22. Tindall, p. 126.

23. Beechhold, p. 5, and Adaline Glasheen, *A Third Census of Finnegans Wake* (Berkeley: University of California Press, 1977), p. 92. *Cumhal* also meant a handmaid or female slave and served as an exchange unit (for payment of blood fines) worth three cows. Cf. "serebanmaids" (126.19), from which *fionn cumhal* may be derived: modern Irish *ban* = white = *fionn;* maids = *cumhal*. (My thanks to Professor Janet Dunleavy for calling this pun to my attention.)

24. There is also a reference to Wellington in "Walleslee" (133.21), since Wellington's name was Arthur Wellesley (cf. 137.11: "Juke of Wilysly"). Wellington is probably also the duke in "made the man who had no notion of shopkeepers feel he'd rather play the duke than play the gentleman" (128.15–17), since part of the phrase puns on Napoleon's description of the English as "a nation of shopkeepers" (see Hart, p. 235).

25. There are also some less obvious references to the Park incident (126.18, 128.22, 131.32–33, 132.10, 134.9–11, 134.34–135.4, 138.36–139.2), to stuttering, Earwicker's sign of guilt (139.9), and to the related incidents of the encounter with the Cad and Buckley shooting the Russian General (127.6–7, 137.13–14, 138.13–14).

26. Hayman, pp. 92–93.

27. Other puns include Danish *farfar* and *morfar* (paternal and maternal grandfather): Dounia Bunis Christiani, *Scandinavian Elements of Finnegans Wake* (Evanston: Northwestern University Press, 1965), p. 122. "Far" also puns on Irish *fear*, "man" (pronounced "far"); "morefar" is Irish *fear mor*, "big man."

28. See Hart, pp. 63–64, 134–42.

29. *Letters*, III, 239.

30. Hart, p. 63.

31. Glasheen, *Third Census*, p. xxxix.

32. Hart, p. 121.

33. E.g., "Eelwick" (134.16), "Mr Eelwhipper" (496.12), *"Our Human Conger Eel"* (525.26), "that samesake sibsubstitute of a hooky salmon" (28.35), "and as for the salmon he was coming up in him all life long" (132.35–36), *"an old psalmsobbing lax salmoner"* (525.21), "Way, lungfish! The great fin may cumule!" (525.31); cf. 450.2–20.

34. Campbell and Robinson, p. 108.

35. Hart, pp. 50, 52–53; cf. Campbell and Robinson, p. 340.

36. E. L. Epstein, "Interpreting *Finnegans Wake:* A Half-Way House," *James Joyce Quarterly* 3 (Summer 1966): 267. More recently, Grace Eckley has argued that "the A-O motif of *Finnegans Wake* means continuity rather than polarity" (in Begnal and Eckley, p. 149).

37. Epstein, "Interpreting *Finnegans Wake*," pp. 259–60.

38. Epstein, "Interpreting *Finnegans Wake*," pp. 259–60.

39. The name of Phoenix Park originally had nothing to do with the poenix bird. Joyce wrote to Miss Weaver that "A viceroy who knew no Irish thought this [Phoenix] was the word the Dublin people used and put up the mount of a phoenix in the park. The Irish was *fiunishgue* = clear water from a well of bright water there" (*Letters*, I, 258). Cf. 135.14–15: "changes . . . a well of Artesia into a bird of Arabia."

40. Glasheen, "Notes," p. 7.

41. Brendan O Hehir, *A Gaelic Lexicon for Finnegans Wake* (Berkeley: University of California Press, 1967), p. 89. Eckley notes that Joyce associates the ash with the past (Begnal and Eckley, p. 168).

42. Cf. Hart, pp. 135–42. Although Hart states correctly that in III.3 Shaun and/or

the Donkey lie at the center of the quincunx, Shaun seems primarily to become identified with Christ (and with the Donkey) in the second half of the *Wake,* where he plays out his role as heir apparent to HCE.

43. Hart and Senn, *A Wake Newslitter,* o.s. no. 1 (March 1962), pp. 3-9, and no. 2 (April 1962), pp. 1-5. I have drawn heavily on this excellent study.

44. Hart, p. 81.

45. See, e.g., Ruth von Phul, "Who Sleeps at *Finnegans Wake?*", *James Joyce Review* 1 (June 16, 1957): 27-38; Hart, pp. 78-95; Bernard Benstock, "L. Boom as Dreamer in *Finnegans Wake,*" *PMLA* 82 (March 1967): 91-97, and *Joyce-again's Wake,* p. 215.

46. Michael H. Begnal, "The Dreamers at the Wake: A View of Narration and Point of View," in Begnal and Eckley, pp. 20-26.

47. James S. Atherton, "The Identity of the Sleeper," *A Wake Newslitter* 4 (October 1967): 83-85.

48. Hart, p. 77.

49. "White is twain" may also allude to the two kinds of white references associated with Earwicker: Finn's white hat (Earwicker as native Irishman) and Wellington's white horse (Earwicker as imperialist-invader).

50. Edmund Curtis, *A History of Ireland* (London: Methuen, University Paperbacks, 1961), p. 151.

Chapter 4: The First Riddle of the Universe

1. For more detailed analyses of the Park incident, the encounter with the Cad, and the letter, see Bernard Benstock, "Every Telling Has a Taling: A Reading of the Narrative in *Finnegans Wake,*" *Modern Fiction Studies* 15 (Spring 1969): 3-25.

2. See Northrop Frye, *Fearful Symmetry: A Study of William Blake* (Princeton: Princeton University Press, 1970), pp. 73-74.

3. Archer Taylor, *English Riddles from Oral Tradition* (Berkeley: University of California Press, 1951), pp. 301-3.

4. Taylor, p. 303.

5. *Pindar's Odes,* trans. Roy Arthur Swanson (Indianapolis: Bobbs-Merrill, 1974), p. 110.

6. *James Joyce's Scribbledehobble: The Ur-Workbook for Finnegans Wake,* ed. Thomas E. Connolly (Evanston: Northwestern University Press, 1961), p. 142.

7. *A First-Draft Version of Finnegans Wake,* ed. David Hayman (London: Faber and Faber, 1963), p. 113.

8. The pun on "naughty" and "not a" appears in two later versions of the riddle (495.6, 607.11), in both cases incorporating "nought." Impotence and sexual guilt or perversion are often confused in the *Wake.* As "nought," Earwicker is a zero, one of Joyce's female symbols: note the "O" at the beginning of I.8, ALP as "zeroine" (261.24), and the "zeroic couplet" (284.10).

9. Clive Hart, *Structure and Motif in Finnegans Wake* (Evanston: Northwestern University Press, 1962), p. 130.

10. Hart, p. 131.

11. Benstock, "Every Telling," p. 14.

12. Leo Knuth, "Shem's Riddle of the Universe," *A Wake Newslitter* 9 (October 1972):79.

13. William York Tindall, *A Reader's Guide to Finnegans Wake* (New York: Farrar, Straus and Giroux, 1969), p. 14; see also pp. 132–33.
14. Ovid, *Metamorphoses*, trans. Mary M. Innes (Baltimore: Penguin Books, 1955), p. 184.
15. Margaret C. Solomon, "Sham Rocks: Shem's Answer to the First Riddle of the Universe," *A Wake Newslitter* 7 (October 1970):70–71.
16. Patricia A. Morley, "Fish Symbolism in Chapter Seven of *Finnegans Wake:* The Hidden Defense of Shem the Penman," *James Joyce Quarterly* 6 (Spring 1969):270. Begnal also notes that Shem's riddle "is directed outward, to *any* man, and thus it attempts to make a point about humanity instead of being a further definition of Shem's own character." Michael H. Begnal and Grace Eckley, *Narrator and Character in Finnegans Wake* (Lewisburg, Pa.: Bucknell University Press, 1975), p. 110.
17. Solomon, p. 72.
18. Knuth, "Shem's Riddle of the Universe," p. 88.
19. Knuth, "Shem's Riddle of the Universe," p. 82.
20. Cf. Bernard Benstock, *Joyce-again's Wake* (Seattle: University of Washington Press, 1965), p. 208. The identification is substantiated at 230.35–36, where the home is described as a castle on a once prosperous street, now stone broke.
21. Leo Knuth, "Shem's Riddle of the Universe (continued),"*A Wake Newslitter* 11 (December 1974):98.
22. Hayman, p. 167.
23. Eric Partridge, *A Dictionary of Slang and Unconventional English*, 7th ed. (New York: MacMillan, 1970), p. 477.
24. Hart, pp. 129–34.
25. Note the description of Mr. Dedalus on the first page of the *Portrait:* "his father looked at him through a glass: he had a hairy face." Joseph Campbell and Henry Morton Robinson identify the bearded figure as "God the Father in his aspect of Creator, the Concealed Ancient One from the Strands of Whose Beard the entire world proceeds." *A Skeleton Key to Finnegans Wake* (New York: Viking Compass Edition, 1961), p. 164 n. The description also fits Parnell.
26. Knuth, "Shem's Riddle of the Universe," p. 80.
27. The "nam" also suggests a lack of identity: cf. Latin *namquis*, "anyone at all."
28. Cf. Benstock, *Joyce-again's Wake*, p. 207.

Chapter 5: Who's Who: The Prankquean's Riddle

1. Bernard Benstock, *Joyce-again's Wake* (Seattle: University of Washington Press, 1965), p. 267.
2. Grace Eckley, "'Petween Peas Like Ourselves': The Folklore of the Prankquean," *James Joyce Quarterly* 9 (Winter 1971–72):186.
3. J. Mitchell Morse, "Where Terms Begin," in *A Conceptual Guide to Finnegans Wake*, ed. Michael H. Begnal and Fritz Senn (University Park: Pennsylvania State University Press, 1974), p. 15.
4. Bernard Benstock has suggested to me that Irish porter and German piesporter "provide for both the Irish and Germanic versions" of the Tristan and Iseult myth.
5. Vivian Mercier, *The Irish Comic Tradition* (Oxford: Oxford University Press, 1962), p. 32.

Notes

6. See Eckley's article.

7. Sigmund Freud, "The Occurrence in Dreams of Material from Fairy Tales," trans. James Strachey, in *Delusion and Dream,* ed. Philip Rieff (Boston: Beacon Press, 1956), pp. 134–42.

8. On door symbolism in the *Wake* see Margaret C. Solomon, *Eternal Geomater* (Carbondale: Southern Illinois University Press, 1969), pp. 50–57 et passim.

9. Frank Budgen, *James Joyce and the Making of Ulysses* (Bloomington: Indiana University Press, 1960), p. 209.

10. Richard Ellmann, *James Joyce* (New York: Oxford University Press, 1959), p. 720.

11. *A First-Draft Version of Finnegans Wake,* ed. David Hayman (London: Faber and Faber, 1963), pp. 58–59.

12. Hayman indicates that his reading of "cupss" is doubtful. Perhaps Joyce wrote (or meant to write) "cupsa," as in the first version of the second request for porter.

13. Frances Boldereff, *Hermes to His Son Thoth* (Woodward, Pa.: Classic Nonfiction Library, 1968), p. 107.

14. Benstock, p. 269.

15. Benstock, p. 284; Solomon, p. 12.

16. E. L. Epstein, "Chance, Doubt, Coincidence and the Prankquean's Riddle," *A Wake Newslitter* 6 (February 1969):7.

17. Robert R. Boyle, S.J., *James Joyce's Pauline Version* (Carbondale: Southern Illinois University Press, 1978), p. 109. I am indebted to Father Boyle for several ideas that I have developed in this chapter.

18. William York Tindall, *A Reader's Guide to Finnegans Wake* (New York: Farrar, Straus and Giroux, 1969), p. 47.

19. Solomon, p. 9.

20. Cf. Benstock, pp. 271–72.

21. Michael H. Begnal, "The Prankquean in *Finnegans Wake,*" *James Joyce Quarterly* 1:3 (Spring 1964):16.

22. Begnal, p. 17.

23. Solomon, p. 31.

24. This gloss was also suggested by E. L. Epstein in "Interpreting *Finnegans Wake:* A Half-Way House," *James Joyce Quarterly* 3 (Summer 1966):268.

25. Some evidence (which I have assimilated into my argument) is presented by Begnal, p. 14.

26. Tom Peete Cross and Clark Harris Slover, *Ancient Irish Tales* (New York: Barnes & Noble, 1969), pp. 370–421.

27. Cf. Hugh Kenner, *Dublin's Joyce* (Bloomington: Indiana University Press, 1956), p. 347.

28. Joseph Campbell and Henry Morton Robinson, *A Skeleton Key to Finnegans Wake* (New York: Viking Compass Edition, 1961), p. 52 n.

29. Boyle, p. 20. Father Boyle substantiates his argument by pointing to a number of allusions to religious ritual in the tale. As possible solutions to the riddle he suggests "Because I am consecrated wine" and (p. 21) "Because I am transaccidentated, and all you can see of me is the appearance of wine or, in the chambermade music in which I exist, of urine."

30. Clive Hart, *Structure and Motif in Finnegans Wake* (Evanston: Northwestern University Press, 1962), p. 77.

31. This pun adds an interesting symbolic level to Shem's creation of the written word *(ord)* out of his ordure (27.10-11, 185.14-186.8).

32. Eric Partridge, *A Dictionary of Slang and Unconventional English*, 7th ed. (New York: Macmillan, 1970), p. 402.

33. Ellmann, p. 22.

34. Brendan O Hehir, *A Gaelic Lexicon for Finnegans Wake* (Berkeley: University of California Press, 1967), pp. 403-5. Cf. Campbell and Robinson, p. 200.

35. Solomon, p. 35.

36. Hart, p. 220.

37. Campbell and Robinson, pp. 302-3.

38. Partridge (p. 629) says that the pike-toll is a figure for death, and that "to pike" or "to pike off" is to die.

Chapter 6: Whose Hue: Izod's Heliotrope Riddle

1. M. J. C. Hodgart has noted the importance of Puccini's *Turandot*, in which suitors to the Princess Turandot are required to solve riddles or lose their lives, in connection with this episode. "Music and the Mime of Mick, Nick, and the Maggies," in *A Conceptual Guide to Finnegans Wake*, ed. Michael H. Begnal and Fritz Senn (University Park: Pennsylvania State University Press, 1974), pp. 87-88.

2. *Letters*, I, 295.

3. *Letters*, I, 406.

4. Adaline Glasheen, *A Second Census of Finnegans Wake* (Evanston: Northwestern University Press, 1963), p. xl.

5. "Notes by the Author" appended to *Exiles* (New York: Viking Compass Edition, 1961), p. 113.

6. Margaret C. Solomon, *Eternal Geomater* (Carbondale: Southern Illinois University Press, 1969), pp. 22, 27-28. See also Anthony Burgess, *Re Joyce* (New York: Norton, 1968), p. 221, and Eugene Jolas, "Marginalia to James Joyce's Work in Progress," *Transition*, no. 22 (February 1933), p. 103.

7. Bernard Benstock lists references to the eyepatch in *Joyce-again's Wake* (Seattle: University of Washington Press, 1965), pp. 227-28 n.

8. Clive Hart, *Structure and Motif in Finnegans Wake* (Evanston: Northwestern University Press, 1962), pp. 17, 71-72.

9. Cf. Robert Boyle, S.J., "*Finnegans Wake*, Page 185: An Explication," *James Joyce Quarterly* 4 (Fall 1966):3-16. It is also worth noting that there is a parallel between the treatment of writing in terms of urination here and its treatment in terms of sowing seeds in Stephen's riddle in "Nestor."

10. Adaline Glasheen, *A Third Census of Finnegans Wake* (Berkeley: University of California Press, 1977), pp. l-li.

11. Solomon, p. 23.

12. Joseph Campbell and Henry Morton Robinson, *A Skeleton Key to Finnegans Wake* (New York: Viking Compass Edition, 1961), p. 145.

13. Benstock, pp. xix-xx.

14. E. L. Epstein, "Interpreting *Finnegans Wake*: A Half-Way House," *James Joyce Quarterly* 3 (Summer 1966):256; see *Letters*, I, 154. I am not certain how Epstein knows the band was yellow; it could have been grayish white.

15. Epstein, pp. 255-56.
16. Brendan O Hehir and John Dillon translate "per causes nunsibellies" as *per causas nuntiatas belli*, "through the declared causes of the war." *A Classical Lexicon for Finnegans Wake* (Berkeley: University of California Press, 1977), p. 194.
17. Campbell and Robinson, p. 150 n.
18. Epstein, pp. 255, 271.
19. Solomon, pp. 28-29.
20. Campbell and Robinson, p. 152.
21. Helmut Bonheim, *A Lexicon of the German in Finnegans Wake* (Berkeley: University of California Press, 1967), p. 81.
22. *Chamber Music*, ed. William York Tindall (New York: Columbia University Press, 1954), p. 129. I assume that in the Mime, Shem is the jester-lover depicted in the poem.
23. Epstein, p. 256.
24. Vincent F. Hopper and Gerald B. Lahey, introduction to *The Importance of Being Earnest* (Woodbury, N.Y.: Barron's Educational Series, 1959), p. 36.
25. William York Tindall, *A Reader's Guide to Finnegans Wake* (New York: Farrar, Straus and Giroux, 1969), p. 171.

Conclusion

1. For the last two of these see my article "'Our Wee Free State': *Finnegans Wake* and Irish Independence," *Modern British Literature* 2 (Spring 1977):75-80, and Mark L. Troy, *Mummeries of Resurrection: The Cycle of Osiris in Finnegans Wake*, Acta Universitatis Upsaliensis, Studia Anglistica Upsaliensia 26 (Uppsala, 1976).
2. Bernard Benstock, "The State of the *Wake*," *James Joyce Quarterly* 14 (Spring 1977):238.
3. Margot Norris, *The Decentered Universe of Finnegans Wake* (Baltimore: Johns Hopkins University Press, 1976), p. 91.
4. Samuel Beckett, "Dante . . . Bruno. Vico . . Joyce," in Beckett et al., *Our Exagmination Round His Factification for Incamination of Work in Progress* (New York: New Directions, 1962), p. 14.
5. Richard Ellmann, *James Joyce* (New York: Oxford University Press, 1959), p. 535.
6. Norris, p. 78.
7. Ellmann, p. 648.

Bibliography

I. Primary Sources

Chamber Music. Edited by William York Tindall. New York: Columbia University Press, 1954.

Dubliners. Edited by Robert Scholes in consultation with Richard Ellmann. New York: Viking Compass Edition, 1968.

Exiles. New York: Viking Compass Edition, 1961.

Finnegans Wake. New York: Viking Compass Edition, 1959.

A First-Draft Version of Finnegans Wake. Edited by David Hayman. London: Faber and Faber, 1963.

James Joyce's Scribbledehobble: The Ur-Workbook for Finnegans Wake. Edited by Thomas E. Connolly. Evanston: Northwestern University Press, 1961.

Letters of James Joyce, 3 vols. Vol. I edited by Stuart Gilbert, vols. II and III edited by Richard Ellmann. New York: Viking Press, 1966.

A Portrait of the Artist as a Young Man. Corrected from the Dublin holograph by Chester G. Anderson and edited by Richard Ellmann. New York: Viking Compass Edition, 1964.

Ulysses. New York: Modern Library, 1961.

II. Secondary Sources

Abrahams, Roger D. "The Literary Study of the Riddle." *Texas Studies in Literature and Language* 14 (Spring 1972): 177-97.

Aristotle. *On Poetry and Style.* Translated by G. M. A. Grube. Indianapolis: Library of Liberal Arts, 1958.

Atherton, James S. *The Books at the Wake: A Study of Literary Allusions in James Joyce's Finnegans Wake.* New York: Viking Press, 1960.

———. "The Identity of the Sleeper." *A Wake Newslitter* 4 (October 1967):83-85.
Beckett, Samuel, et al. *Our Exagmination Round His Factification for Incamination of Work in Progress.* New York: New Directions, 1962.
Beechhold, Henry Frank. "Early Irish History and Mythology in *Finnegans Wake.*" Ann Arbor: University Microfilms, 1956.
———. "Finn MacCool and *Finnegans Wake.*" *James Joyce Review* 2 (Spring-Summer 1958):3-12.
Begnal, Michael H. "The Prankquean in *Finnegans Wake.*" *James Joyce Quarterly* 1:3 (Spring 1964):14-18.
Begnal, Michael H., and Grace Eckley. *Narrator and Character in Finnegans Wake.* Lewisburg, Pa.: Bucknell University Press, 1975.
Begnal, Michael H., and Fritz Senn, eds. *A Conceptual Guide to Finnegans Wake.* University Park: Pennsylvania State University Press, 1974.
Benstock, Bernard. "Every Telling Has a Taling: A Reading of the Narrative in *Finnegans Wake.*" *Modern Fiction Studies* 15 (Spring 1969):3-25.
———. *Joyce-again's Wake: An Analysis of Finnegans Wake.* Seattle: University of Washington Press, 1965.
———. "L. Boom as Dreamer in *Finnegans Wake.*" *PMLA* 82 (March 1967):91-97.
———. "The State of the *Wake.*" *James Joyce Quarterly* 14 (Spring 1977):237-40.
Boldereff, Frances M. *Hermes to His Son Thoth: Being Joyce's Use of Giordano Bruno in Finnegans Wake.* Woodward, Pa.: Classic Non-fiction Library, 1968.
Bonheim, Helmut. *A Lexicon of the German in Finnegans Wake.* Berkeley: University of California Press, 1967.
Bowen, Zack. *Musical Allusions in the Works of James Joyce: Early Poetry through Ulysses.* Albany: State University of New York Press, 1974.
Boyle, Robert, S.J. "*Finnegans Wake,* Page 185: An Explication." *James Joyce Quarterly* 4 (Fall 1966):3-16.
———. *James Joyce's Pauline Vision: A Catholic Exposition.* Carbondale: Southern Illinois University Press, 1978.
Brown, Waln K. "Cognitive Ambiguity and the 'Pretended Obscene Riddle.'" *Keystone Folklore Quarterly* 18 (1973):89-101.
Budgen, Frank. *James Joyce and the Making of Ulysses.* Bloomington: Indiana University Press, 1960.
Burgess, Anthony. "If Oedipus Had Read His Lévi-Strauss." In *Urgent Copy: Literary Studies.* New York: Norton, 1968.

———. *Re Joyce*. New York: Norton, 1968.
Campbell, Joseph, and Henry Morton Robinson. *A Skeleton Key to Finnegans Wake*. New York: Viking Compass Edition, 1961.
Christiani, Dounia Bunis. *Scandinavian Elements of Finnegans Wake*. Evanston: Northwestern University Press, 1965.
Cowan, Thomas A. "Sacer Esto?" *A Wake Newslitter* 11 (June 1974): 39–44.
Cross, Tom Peete. *Motif-Index of Early Irish Literature*. Bloomington: Indiana University Press, 1952.
Cross, Tom Peete, and Clark Harris Slover, eds. *Ancient Irish Tales*. New York: Barnes & Noble, 1969.
Curtis, Edmund. *A History of Ireland*. London: Methuen, University Paperbacks, 1961.
Dundes, Alan. "The Study of Folklore in Literature and Culture: Identification and Interpretation." *Journal of American Folklore* 78 (April–June 1965):136–42.
Eckley, Grace. "'Petween Peas Like Ourselves': The Folklore of the Prankquean." *James Joyce Quarterly* 9 (Winter 1971–72):177–88.
Ellmann, Richard. *James Joyce*. New York: Oxford University Press, 1959.
Epstein, E. L. "Chance, Doubt, Coincidence and the Prankquean's Riddle." *A Wake Newslitter* 6 (February 1969):3–7.
———. "Interpreting *Finnegans Wake*: A Half-Way House." *James Joyce Quarterly* 3 (Summer 1966):252–71.
Flower, Robin. *The Irish Tradition*. Oxford: Oxford University Press, 1947.
Freud, Sigmund. "The Occurrence in Dreams of Material from Fairy Tales." Translated by James Strachey. In *Delusion and Dream* edited by Philip Rieff. Boston: Beacon Press, 1956.
Frye, Northrop. *Fearful Symmetry: A Study of William Blake*. Princeton: Princeton University Press, 1970.
Gilbert, Stuart. *James Joyce's Ulysses: A Study*. New ed. New York: Vintage Books, 1952.
Glasheen, Adaline. "Notes Towards a Supreme Understanding of the Use of 'Finnegan's Wake' in *Finnegans Wake*." *A Wake Newslitter* 5 (February 1968):4–15.
———. "Part of What the Thunder Said in *Finnegans Wake*." *Analyst*, no. 23 (November 1964), pp. 1–29.
———. *A Second Census of Finnegans Wake*. Evanston: Northwestern University Press, 1963.
———. *A Third Census of Finnegans Wake*. Berkeley: University of California Press, 1977.

Graves, Robert. *The Greek Myths.* Rev. ed. 2 vols. Baltimore: Penguin Books, 1960.
Hart, Clive. *A Concordance to Finnegans Wake.* Minneapolis: University of Minnesota Press, 1963.
———. *Structure and Motif in Finnegans Wake.* Evanston: Northwestern University Press, 1962.
Hart, Clive, and Fritz Senn. "EXPLICATIONS—for the greeter glossary of code." *A Wake Newslitter,* o.s. no. 1 (March 1962), pp. 3-9; no. 2 (April 1962), pp. 1-5.
Hopper, Vincent F., and Gerald B. Lahey. Introduction to *The Importance of Being Earnest* by Oscar Wilde. Woodbury, N.Y.: Barron's Educational Series, 1959.
Howarth, Herbert. *The Irish Writers 1880-1940: Literature under Parnell's Star.* London: Rockliff, 1958.
Huizinga, Johan. *Homo Ludens: A Study of the Play-Element in Culture.* New York: Roy Publishers, 1950.
Hull, Vernam, and Archer Taylor. *A Collection of Irish Riddles.* Berkeley: University of California Press, 1955.
Jolas, Eugene. "Marginalia to James Joyce's Work in Progress." *Transition,* no. 22 (February 1933), pp. 101-5.
Kenner, Hugh. *Dublin's Joyce.* Bloomington: Indiana University Press, 1956.
Knuth, Leo. "Shem's Riddle of the Universe." *A Wake Newslitter* 9 (October 1972):79-89.
———. "Shem's Riddle of the Universe (continued)." *A Wake Newslitter* 11 (December 1974):93-103.
Lévi-Strauss, Claude. *The Scope of Anthropology.* Translated by Sherry Ortner Paul and Robert A. Paul. London: Jonathan Cape, 1967.
Litz, A. Walton. *The Art of James Joyce: Method and Design in Ulysses and Finnegans Wake.* Corrected edition. New York: Oxford University Press, 1964.
MacManus, M. J. *Eamon de Valera: A Biography.* Dublin: Talbot Press, 1944.
McCall, P. J. "Folk Lore Riddles—Irish and Anglo-Irish." *Journal of the National Literary Society of Ireland* 1:2 (1900):61-80.
McCarthy, Patrick A. "Allusions in *Ulysses:* Random Addenda and Corrigenda for Thornton." *James Joyce Quarterly* 13 (Fall 1975):53-59.
———. "'Our Wee Free State': *Finnegans Wake* and Irish Independence." *Modern British Literature* 2 (Spring 1977):75-80.
McHugh, Roland. *The Sigla of Finnegans Wake.* Austin: University of Texas Press, 1976.

Mercier, Vivian. "In the Wake of the Fianna: Some Additions and Corrections to Glasheen and a Footnote or Two to Atherton." In *A James Joyce Miscellany, Third Series,* edited by Marvin Magalaner. Carbondale: Southern Illinois University Press, 1962.

───. *The Irish Comic Tradition.* Oxford: Oxford University Press, 1962.

Morley, Patricia A. "Fish Symbolism in Chapter Seven of *Finnegans Wake:* The Hidden Defense of Shem the Penman." *James Joyce Quarterly* 6 (Spring 1969):267-70.

Norris, Margot. *The Decentered Universe of Finnegans Wake: A Structuralist Approach.* Baltimore: Johns Hopkins University Press, 1976.

O Hehir, Brendan. *A Gaelic Lexicon for Finnegans Wake.* Berkeley: University of California Press, 1967.

O Hehir, Brendan, and John Dillon. *A Classical Lexicon for Finnegans Wake.* Berkeley: University of California Press, 1977.

Ovid. *Metamorphoses.* Translated by Mary M. Innes. Baltimore: Penguin Books, 1955.

Partridge, Eric. *A Dictionary of Slang and Unconventional English.* 7th ed. New York: Macmillan, 1970.

Peachy, Frederic, ed. *Clareti Enigmata: The Latin Riddles of Claret.* Berkeley: University of California Press, 1957.

Pindar. *Pindar's Odes.* Translated by Roy Arthur Swanson. Indianapolis: Bobbs-Merrill, 1974.

Robinson, Fred Norris. *Satirists and Enchanters in Early Irish Literature.* American Committee for Irish Studies: Reprints in Irish Studies, no. 1, n.d. Reprinted from *Studies in the History of Religions,* ed. David Gordon Lyon and George Foot Moore. New York, 1912.

Schutte, William M. *Joyce and Shakespeare: A Study in the Meaning of Ulysses.* New Haven: Yale University Press, 1957.

Skrabanek, Petr. "Structure and Motif in Thunderwords: A Proposal." *A Wake Newslitter* 12 (December 1975): 108-11.

Solomon, Margaret C. *Eternal Geomater: The Sexual Universe of Finnegans Wake.* Carbondale: Southern Illinois University Press, 1969.

───. "Sham Rocks: Shem's Answer to the First Riddle of the Universe." *A Wake Newslitter* 7 (October 1970):67-73.

Stokes, Whitley. "Irish Riddles." *Celtic Review* 1 (1904):132-35.

Swanson, Roy Arthur. "Edible Wandering Rocks: The Pun as Allegory in Joyce's 'Lestrygonians.'" *Genre* 5 (December 1972):385-403.

Swinson, Ward. "Riddles in *Finnegans Wake.*" *Twentieth Century Literature* 19 (July 1973):165-80.

Taylor, Archer. *English Riddles from Oral Tradition.* Berkeley: University of California Press, 1951.

———. *The Literary Riddle Before 1600.* Berkeley: University of California Press, 1948.

Thompson, Stith. *Motif-Index of Folk-Literature.* Rev. ed. 6 vols. Bloomington: Indiana University Press, 1966.

Thornton, Weldon. *Allusions in Ulysses: An Annotated List.* Chapel Hill: University of North Carolina Press, 1968.

Tindall, William York. "James Joyce and the Hermetic Tradition." *Journal of the History of Ideas* 15 (January 1954):23-39.

———. *A Reader's Guide to Finnegans Wake.* New York: Farrar, Straus and Giroux, 1969.

———. *A Reader's Guide to James Joyce.* New York: Farrar, Straus and Giroux, 1959.

Troy, Mark L. *Mummeries of Resurrection: The Cycle of Osiris in Finnegans Wake.* Uppsala: Acta Universitatis Upsaliensis, 1976.

Unkeless, Elaine. "Bats and Sanguivorous Bugaboos." *James Joyce Quarterly* 15 (Winter 1978):128-33.

Vico, Giambattista. *The New Science of Giambattista Vico,* Abridged Translation of the Third Edition (1744). Translated and edited by Thomas Goddard Bergin and Max Harold Fisch. Ithaca: Cornell University Press, 1970.

von Phul, Ruth. "Who Sleeps at *Finnegans Wake?*" *James Joyce Review* 1 (June 16, 1957):27-38.

Worthington, Mabel P. "Nursery Rhymes in *Finnegans Wake.*" *Journal of American Folklore* 70 (January-March, 1957):37-48.

Index

(References to critics in the notes are indexed only when there are no corresponding references in the main text.)

Abrahams, Roger D., 158 n. 29, 159 n. 2
Adam and Eve. See Fall of Man
Aristotle, 17, 157 n. 7
Atherton, James S., 56, 72
Athy's riddle, 18, 25, 33, 141

Becket, Thomas à, 59–60
Beckett, Samuel, 154
Beechhold, Henry Frank, 30, 56, 162 n. 23
Begnal, Michael H., 72, 114–15, 164 n. 16, 165 n. 25
Benoïst-Méchin, Jacques, 154
Benstock, Bernard, 55, 86, 105, 112, 146–47, 153, 158 n. 13, 160 n. 1, 161 n. 11, 163 n. 45, 163 n. 1, 164 n. 20, 164 n. 28, 164 n. 4, 165 n. 15, 165 n. 20, 166 n. 7
Beowulf, 118
Blake, William, 26, 80
Bloom's riddles: "Where was Moses ...," 18, 34, 45, 157 n. 12; "Brothers and sisters ...," 19, 34, 40, 45. See also *Rose of Castille* riddle
Böhme, Jakob, 90
Boldereff, Frances M., 111, 112
Bonheim, Helmut, 149

Boru, Brian, 57
Bowen, Zack, 160 n. 15, 160 n. 16
Boyle, Robert, S.J., 112, 120, 165 n. 17, 165 n. 29, 166 n. 9
"Bricriu's Feast," 118
Brown, Waln K., 159 n. 2
Bruno, Giordano, 112
Budgen, Frank, 16, 110, 137, 157 n. 6
Burgess, Anthony, 166 n. 6; *MF* 27
Burrus and Caseous, 51, 52–53, 161 n. 11
Byrne, J.F., 17

Cad, encounter with, 79, 86, 87–88, 91, 162 n. 25, 163 n. 1
Campbell, Joseph, and Henry Morton Robinson, 16, 23, 52, 67, 120, 147, 148, 162 n. 35, 164 n. 25, 166 n. 37, 166 n. 12, 167 n. 17
Christiani, Dounia Bunis, 162 n. 27
Claret, 25, 157 n. 12
Clontarf, Battle of, 31, 57, 117
Collideorscape riddle, 32, 48, 50, 51–52, 54, 71–77, 99
Cohn, Alan M., 160 n. 10
Coleridge, Samuel T., *The Rime of the Ancient Mariner* 129
Colum, Mary, 156

Index

Colum, Padraic, 156
Connolly, Thomas E., 163 n. 6
Cowan, Thomas A., 161 n. 5
Cross, Tom Peete, 118, 158 n. 32, 159 n. 34
Cuchulain, 27, 118–19
Curtis, Edmund, 74

Daedalus, 30, 89
Dermot and Grania myth, 56–57, 108, 117, 118
Dillon, John, 167 n. 16
Dundes, Alan, 40
Dunleavy, Janet, 145, 162 n. 23

Eckley, Grace, 105, 161 n. 10, 162 n. 36, 162 n. 41, 165 n. 6
Ellmann, Richard, 125, 159 n. 46, 165 n. 10, 167 n. 5, 167 n. 7
Epstein, E.L., 68, 112, 120, 147–48, 150, 161 n. 5, 165 n. 24
Eucharistic symbolism 23, 62, 66, 70–71, 92, 120–21, 130, 131–32, 134
Eunuch riddle, 24, 81

Fall of Man (Garden of Eden story), 17, 59, 69, 71, 79–80, 83–84, 87, 91, 93, 94, 95, 96–97, 98–99, 106, 111–12, 116, 117, 130, 136, 140, 143. *See also* Park incident
Feuerstein, V.R., 146
"Finnegan's Wake" (song), 17, 52, 56, 63, 70, 114
Finn MacCool, 17, 21, 27, 51, 53, 56–57, 58, 66, 108, 118, 126, 162 n. 23, 163 n. 49
Finn MacCool riddle, 21, 24, 29, 32, 48, 51, 53, 54–63, 76
First riddle of the universe. *See* Shem's riddle
Flower, Robin, 159 n. 41
Freud, Sigmund, 101, 109–10
Frye, Northrop, 163 n. 2

Gaelic riddles, 30
Galileo, 31
Gilbert, Stuart, 160 n. 13

Glasheen, Adaline, 23, 31, 65, 139, 143, 158 n. 19, 158 n. 20, 160 n. 7, 161 n. 4, 162 n. 23
Graves, Robert, 157 n. 10

Hart, Clive, 51, 55, 64, 72, 73, 85, 130, 141, 161 n. 8, 162 n. 24, 162 n. 28, 162 n. 32, 162 n. 35, 162 n. 42, 163 n. 45, 164 n. 24, 165 n. 30
Hayman, David, 55, 62, 112, 161 n. 15, 163 n. 7, 164 n. 22, 165 n. 12
Heliotrope riddle, 27, 32, 47, 106, 115, 123, 136–52
Henry II, 57, 59
Heresy, 83, 89–90
Hodgart, M.J.C., 166 n. 1
Homer: *The Odyssey*, 18, 31, 82; *The Iliad*, 117, 118
Hopper, Vincent F., 167 n. 24
Howarth, Herbert, 16
Huizinga, Johan, 26, 30
Hull, Vernam, 20, 157 n. 9, 158 n. 14, 160 n. 11
Humpty Dumpty riddle, 17, 21–23, 25, 128

Ibsen, Henrik: *The Master Builder*, 62–63; *When We Dead Awaken*, 87
Incest, 36, 37–40, 41, 46, 61, 96, 101, 103, 108, 109, 110, 112, 124, 128, 131, 140, 147; and riddling, 27–29
Irish capitol city riddle, 32, 48, 49–50, 52, 53, 63–72, 76–77
"Is life worth living?" (riddle), 18–19, 24
Isaac, 88, 97
"I've Been Working on the Railroad," 50

Jaun's riddle, 24
Jolas, Eugene, 166 n. 6
Joyce, James, other works by: *Chamber Music*, 149; *Exiles*, 140–41; *A Portrait of the Artist as a Young Man*, 18, 25–26, 33, 54, 83, 89, 95, 141, 150, 155; *Scribbledehobble*

(notebook), 82; "The Sisters," 94; "Two Gallants," 42; *Ulysses,* 16-17, 18, 19, 26, 32, 33-46, 47-48, 49, 50, 54, 71, 80, 81, 82, 83, 88, 92, 98, 102, 103, 109, 112, 141, 150, 153, 154-55
Joyce, John, 125
Joyce, Nora, 15

Kenner, Hugh, 160 n. 3, 165 n. 27
Knuth, Leo, 87, 92, 94, 97, 102

Lahey, Gerald B., 167 n. 24
Lenehan's riddle. *See Rose of Castille* riddle
Letter in *Finnegans Wake,* 22, 47-48, 55, 80, 83, 89, 92, 94, 95, 100, 121, 122-23, 143, 154
Lévi-Strauss, Claude, 27-28
Lilith, 108
Litz, A. Walton, 161 n. 18
Louys, Pierre, *Aphrodite,* 150

MacManus, M.J., 158 n. 17
McCall, P.J., 160 n. 10
McCann, Philip, 125
McHugh, Roland, 161 n. 11, 161 n. 15
Mercier, Vivian, 20, 24, 27, 108, 159 n. 41, 159 n. 42
Milligan, Alice, *The Last Feast of the Fianna,* 56-57
Milton, John, 80; *Lycidas,* 36; *Paradise Lost,* 140; *Paradise Regained,* 119
M'Intosh, 34, 46
Mirror riddle ("nobody and somebody"), 24, 81-82
Molly's riddle, 34, 159 n. 2
Mookse and the Gripes, 51, 52, 88
Moore, Thomas, "The Last Rose of Summer," 43, 44
Morley, Patricia A., 164 n. 16
Morse, J. Mitchell, 105
Murray, Josephine, 16

Newton, Isaac, 59
Noah, 61, 69
Norris, Margot, 154
Norwegian Captain, 125-29, 135

"Och Johnny I Hardly Knew Ye," 60
O'Connell, Daniel, 69-70
Oedipus, 27, 28, 100-101, 108, 124, 129. *See also* Incest; Sphinx's riddle
O Hehir, Brendan, 162 n. 41, 166 n. 34, 167 n. 16
O'Malley, Grace, 57, 107, 121, 122, 133
Onan story, 110
Ondt and the Gracehoper, 87, 131
Ovid, *Metamorphoses,* 38, 159 n. 6, 164 n. 14

Park incident, 22, 28-29, 53, 60-61, 68-69, 79-80, 84, 86, 87, 91, 92-93, 97, 98, 99-100, 107, 110, 111, 121, 122-23, 126, 127, 128-30, 132, 138-39, 142-43, 151-52, 162 n. 25, 163 n. 1
Parnell, Charles Stewart, 17, 22, 164 n. 25
Partridge, Eric, 98, 124, 166 n. 38
Patrick, St., 25, 138, 145
Peachy, Frederic, 157 n. 12, 158 n. 25, 158 n. 26
Persian riddles, 27
Pigott, Richard, 22, 143
Pindar, 82
Plato, 99
Pound, Ezra, 64
Poynings' Law, 74
Prankquean's riddle, 26, 27, 28, 32, 47, 49, 57, 101, 105-35, 136-37
Prout, Father, "The Bells of Shandon," 49, 52, 67
Puccini, *Turandot,* 166 n. 1
Pyrrha and Deucalion myth, 37-38
Pyrrhus, 35, 37, 40

Riddles, types of, 17-21; as tests, 26-27, 106, 136-37, 140-41, 166 n. 1. *See also* Athy's riddle; Bloom's riddles; Claret; Collideorscape riddle; Eunuch riddle; Finn MacCool riddle; Gaelic riddles; Galileo; Heliotrope riddle; Humpty Dumpty riddle; Incest and riddling; Irish

capitol city riddle; "Is life worth living?"; Jaun's riddle; Mirror riddle; Molly's riddle; Persian riddles; Prankquean's riddle; *Rose of Castille* riddle; Rumpelstiltskin; Samson's riddle; Shem's riddle; Spelling riddles; Sphinx's riddle; Stephen's riddles; Triads
Robinson, Fred Norris, 26
Robinson, Henry Morton. See Campbell, Joseph
Rose of Castille riddle, 18, 33, 42–45, 141
Rumpelstiltskin (riddler), 31, 108–9, 124
Russian General (Butt and Taff story), 22–23, 99, 138, 162 n. 25

Samson's riddle, 19
Schutte, William M., 40, 41
Senn, Fritz, 51, 72
Shakespeare, William, 41; *Hamlet* 41, 76; *The Merchant of Venice* 27, 82; *Romeo and Juliet* 44, 160 n. 17
Shanameh, 27
Shem's riddle, 24, 26, 29, 32, 47, 73, 78–104, 105, 106, 145
Skrabanek, Petr, 158 n. 20
Slover, Clark Harris, 118, 159 n. 34
Solomon, Margaret, 90, 92, 114, 115, 128, 141, 145, 148, 160 n. 1, 165 n. 8, 165 n. 15
Spenser, Edmund, *The Faerie Queene,* 18
Spelling riddles, 24, 114–15, 142–43
Sphinx's riddle, 18, 21, 24–25, 27, 28, 31, 73, 129, 157 n. 9, 157 n. 10
Stephen's riddles: Pier riddle, 35–36, 37, 38; Writing riddle, 36–39, 41, 166 n. 9; Tax riddle, 19, 39–41, 109, 160 n. 10; General references, 26, 33, 42, 141
Stokes, Whitley, 20
Svevo, Italo, 147
Swanson, Roy Arthur, 38, 163 n. 5
Sweeney, James Johnson, 111
Swinson, Ward, 25, 158 n. 13, 159 n. 3

Synge, John M., *Riders to the Sea,* 75

Taylor, Archer, 18, 19–20, 23, 26–27, 30, 37, 157 n. 9, 157 n. 11, 158 n. 14, 158 n. 18, 158 n. 23, 160 n. 11, 163 n. 3, 163 n. 4
Thompson, Stith, 158 n. 32, 159 n. 33
Thornton, Weldon, 20, 36–37, 39, 40
Tindall, William York, 31, 33, 51, 58, 89, 113–14, 151, 159 n. 37
Tiresias, 82
Tom Tit Tot, 124
Tone, Wolfe, 60
Tree and stone, 59, 85–86, 150, 161 n. 10
Triads, 20–21, 158 n. 17
Trinity, 21, 62, 92, 112, 119–21, 131–32
Tristan and Iseult myth, 59, 85, 108, 151, 164 n. 4
Troy, Mark L., 167 n. 1
Twain, Mark, *Huckleberry Finn,* 157 n. 12

Unkeless, Elaine, 160 n. 14

Vico, Giambattista (Viconian theory of history), 31, 51–54, 56, 60, 65, 67, 68, 94, 99, 102, 117–19, 120, 131, 151
Von Phul, Ruth, 163 n. 45

Weaver, Harriet Shaw, 15, 32, 55, 137, 162 n. 39
Wellington, Duke of ("Willingdone"), 58–59, 60–61, 86, 147, 162 n. 24, 163 n. 49
Wells, H.G., 16
Wilde, Oscar, 150; *The Importance of Being Earnest,* 150
"The Wooing of Olwen," 56
Worthington, Mabel P., 158 n. 19

Yeats, William Butler, 87; "When You Are Old," 87
"Yes, We Have No Bananas," 87